Coaching Innovations

Coaching Innovations

Providing Instructional Support Anywhere, Anytime

Edited by Debbie Dailey
and Patty Kohler-Evans

ROWMAN & LITTLEFIELD
Lanham • Boulder • New York • London

Published by Rowman & Littlefield
A wholly owned subsidiary of
The Rowman & Littlefield Publishing Group, Inc.
4501 Forbes Boulevard, Suite 200, Lanham, Maryland 20706
https://rowman.com

Unit A, Whitacre Mews, 26-34 Stannary Street, London SE11 4AB,
United Kingdom

Copyright © 2017 by Debbie Dailey and Patty Kohler-Evans

All rights reserved. No part of this book may be reproduced in any form or by any electronic or mechanical means, including information storage and retrieval systems, without written permission from the publisher, except by a reviewer who may quote passages in a review.

British Library Cataloguing in Publication Information Available

Library of Congress Cataloging-in-Publication Data

Includes bibliographic references.
ISBN 978-1-4758-3297-6 (cloth : alk. paper)
ISBN 978-1-4758-3298-3 (pbk. : alk. paper)
ISBN 978-1-4758-3299-0 (electronic)

∞ ™ The paper used in this publication meets the minimum requirements of American National Standard for Information Sciences Permanence of Paper for Printed Library Materials, ANSI/NISO Z39.48-1992.

Printed in the United States of America

Contents

Foreword   vii

Preface   ix

Introduction   xi
    Debbie Dailey and Patty Kohler-Evans

Section I: Instructional Coaching as an Educational Practice

1. Essential Coaching Skills   3
Patty Kohler-Evans, EdD, University of Central Arkansas
2. Coaching for Affective Development   11
Candice Dowd Barnes, EdD, University of Central Arkansas

Section II: Coaching Teacher Candidates

3. LEAP into Mentoring Teacher Candidates   21
Nancy P. Gallavan, PhD, University of Central Arkansas
4. A Triad of Instructional Coaching: Changing Classroom Practices   31
Michelle Buchanan, MAT, NBCT, University of Central Arkansas
5. Virtual Coaching of Teacher Candidates: Using BIE to Supervise and Support Interns in a Teacher Preparation Program   43
Tammy R. Benson, EdD, University of Central Arkansas

Section III: Coaching Practicing Teachers

6	From Students to Teachers: University Faculty Coaching Novice Teachers *Donna Wake, EdD, and Victoria Groves-Scott, EdD, University of Central Arkansas*	55
7	Coaching to Improve Teachers' Instructional Practices *Debbie Dailey, EdD, University of Central Arkansas*	67
8	Coaching for Arts Integration: Arkansas A+ *Rachelle Miller, PhD, University of Central Arkansas*	75
9	Embedded Professional Development: Virtually Coaching Classroom Teachers *Nykela Jackson, PhD, University of Central Arkansas*	85

Conclusion: Taking Next Steps: A Look to the Future 93
  Patty Kohler-Evans and Debbie Dailey

References 97

About the Editors 103

About the Contributors 105

Foreword

"Superman can fly high way up in the sky, 'cause we believe he can." This set of powerful lyrics was sung by the late and great Luther Vandross. This is not just the beginning of a meaningful song by a velvet crooner but a statement speaking to the very essence of believability. As an experienced coach with multiple skillsets, including athletics as well as the art of teaching, I know it takes tremendous believability in one's own talent in order to transfer that belief pattern to another.

The education field is one of the few remaining walks of life in which the measure of success can be totally attributed to the influence of the coach. Good coaches know exactly how to begin with a deep understanding of the background of those they coach. Let us face it, people of all ages and backgrounds want to know if they are listening to someone who knows their stuff, and, equally important, that they are being listened to. Nevertheless, the good coach also knows to support the flow of energy by exposing the inevitable pitfalls, mistakes, breakdowns, and breakthroughs that help account for effective application of new strategies or techniques. As the relationship between the coach and the one being coached grows, new mistakes are made and evaluated with genuine guidance, while the same strategies are modified for effective application resulting in instant believability.

Communicating a powerful belief in another is not an exact science but an art, a fine art with a seasoning of science mixed with it. Very astute coaches realize this early enough within the craft, and they welcome the evolution of those they coach and how they translate and personalize through invigorating dialogue with plenty of self-reflection, sharing of experiences and honest critique. There are those coaches who think the relationship between coach and coached has to be one of a superior and an underling, when in fact the partnership is much more impactful because the coach learns from the learner and about the learner, resulting in strengthened guidance being given by the coach.

In the seasoned coaching relationship, both coach and learner peer into the learner's personality for his or her natural talents. The coach can then offer constructive tactics to apply via the learner's talents. There is nothing like someone feeling confident that what he or she does well, naturally, can be applied to acquiring a new skill. This is especially important for improving one's teaching and remediation acumen. Confidence level is crucial for new teachers, regardless of how their attempts result in steady progress. Yet the believability to push beyond the early toils increases each time the coach can point out successes that truly speak to the learner's go-to talent. Be it natural, newly absorbed, or gained through practice, the development of one's talents to a skillset is paramount to, again, believability.

In my best coaching relationships, there is a genuine display of my personality, which also happens to be my Personality Mantra, an affirmation tagline that keeps my personality display in realignment. Star athletes formulate something similar when they need to gather themselves within the heat of competition. My Personality Mantra is simply *Coach Yourself*, yet it has some real breadth to it. Over time, I realized that this was one of my most successful coaching approaches, which is to sometimes not coach at all!

The confidence in this approach is gained from the steadfast work and rigorous cultivation of techniques from coaching like that of an athlete having to eventually put the drills learned in strenuous coaching sessions to good use by just getting out there to play. The coach has to model confidence in his or her own coaching relationships by supporting the coached to a certain plateau before gently reminding the new teacher to coach him- or herself. Of course, this encouragement marks a level of growth for the relationship that allows the coaching to transition to more indirect instruction, such as periodic follow-ups and virtual share sessions.

The Luther Vandross song including those believable lyrics about Superman is titled "Make Me a Believer." This is a fitting phrase for the new teacher who begins his or her journey with this very direct request from the survivors of the blazed trail of teaching. Only the believers can transmit their genuine believability to a classroom full of young people who implore the very same direct request. Coupling talent with skills obtained through effective coaching promotes the notion that many people do not mind working hard at something, as long as it is not hard work. This makes them believable coaches.

Todd Parker
CEO, Parker Education and Development
Author of *Success Favors Well-Prepared Teachers*

Preface

According to the International Coaching Foundation (ICF) Code of Ethics, coaching is "partnering with clients in a thought-provoking and creative process that inspires them to maximize their personal and professional potential." An individual has only to read through the words once or twice to see the powerful potential in developing a quality coaching relationship. Partnership implies that there are two co-equals in the relationship. There is no superordinate; there is no subordinate.

Coaching necessitates trust, respect, integrity, commitment, care, and honesty. Quality coaching encourages both the coach and the one being coached to engage in deep reflection about the conversations they share. As one authority has said, the conversation is the relationship. Another powerful component of the coaching definition is the notion of personal and professional potential. Within the coaching relationship magic happens. Both the coach and the one being coached seem to grow in amazing ways, both personally and professionally.

The editors of this book have both been engaged in the art and practice of coaching for a number of years. As seasoned educators, each has taken a different, yet parallel journey to come together and seek to collect a variety of coaching applications. The result is a broad collection of coaching ideas presented through a vast array of settings, while offering some fresh and novel ideas for taking the foundational coaching skills and giving readers numerous examples of various coaching scenarios. While collecting these amazing applications of coaching innovations, the authors sought to ensure that foundational coaching essence was lifted out and presented.

The weaving of virtual and face-to-face coaching both with undergraduate and graduate candidates as well as practicing teachers and other educators gives this book a richness of coaching resources. Readers will quickly note that, whether they are serving as teachers, supervisors, university faculty, or in another capacity, there is something here to meet their needs. In the current climate of educational practice that is both efficient and effective, *Coaching Innovations: Providing Instructional Support Anywhere, Anytime* will provide those interested in instructional improvement through coaching some insightful nuggets to try, adapt, or even adopt as their own.

Introduction

Debbie Dailey and Patty Kohler-Evans

Practicing teachers and teacher candidates need support and guidance as they begin their teaching career and as they integrate new strategies into their teaching repertoire. Teacher and teacher candidate instructional support should focus on classroom content, relate to teachers' current practices, and this support should occur over a sustained time period. To provide this type of support, teacher preparation programs, schools, and professional development providers should consider incorporating a coaching model.

By utilizing a coach, teachers can practice authentic instruction, make informed instructional decisions, and increase their own self-efficacy for teaching with the help of another peer or expert, thereby providing an optimal, risk-free learning environment. Evidence supports the effect of coaching on teaching instruction. Benefits from coaching include positive changes in instructional behavior, increased teaching self-confidence, and improved student learning.

This chapter will define coaching, discuss different coaching models and types of support that coaches can provide, and detail the benefits of coaching including effects on the brain. In conclusion, this chapter will present the purpose and context for the book and provide a brief glimpse of the three sections that comprise the book.

COACHING DEFINED

Coaching is defined as a practice to help teachers transfer newly acquired learning and skills from the *workshop* to the classroom (Showers and Joyce, 1996) using a confidential process in which professional colleagues work to improve various aspects of their teaching (Robbins, 1991). Coaching occurs when two educators share planning, teaching, and evaluating responsibilities through a natural, collaborative support system.

Joyce and Showers (1995) closely examined what makes teachers take what they were learning from professional development activities and actually apply newly learned skills to the classroom. These researchers found that providing information alone resulted in little change in the classroom. It was not until coaching was added to the presentation of information, theory, demonstration, and even practice with feedback that teachers demonstrated a dramatic transfer of training.

One of the most widely recognized authorities on instructional coaching, Jim Knight (2007), describes coaching as a partnership approach to improving instruction. Knight's emphasis on both the coach and the one being coached as co-equals is foundational to his pivotal work in the field of coaching. Targeting the relationship as key, Knight identifies several principles that must be in any effective coaching relationship: equality, choice, voice, dialogue, reflection, praxis, and reciprocity.

The partnership philosophy espoused by Knight (2007, 2011) is instrumental to effective coaching. According to Knight (2011), "When coaches and teachers interact equally as partners, good things happen" (p. 18). In response, teachers often rate interactions with coaches as contributing the most to their instructional changes.

COACHING MODELS

Ackland (1991) describes two types of coaching models: (1) expert, which utilizes an individual with acknowledged expertise to observe, support, and provide feedback to the teacher and (2) reciprocal, which involves at least two teachers who observe and exchange feedback with one another. Coaching with an expert could involve an outside person, such as a university professor, who acts as a mentor for teachers implementing new strategies, curriculum, or content.

Additionally, experts could be instructional specialists at the same school as the teacher. As you will see later in this book, this can be accomplished face-to-face or in a virtual environment. Conversely, reciprocal coaching often involves two teachers who utilize their planning period to observe and give feedback to each other. In this case, both the observing teacher and the teacher being observed benefit from this exchange through the practice of modeling, evaluating, and giving feedback.

SUPPORT PROVIDED BY COACHES

Swafford et al. (1997) recognize three kinds of support provided by coaches: (1) procedural, (2) affective, and (3) reflective. Procedural support involves instructional and classroom management practices, whereas affective support offers teachers reassurance and confirmation in their teaching practices. Reflective support allows teachers time to consider the vision of future lessons and what changes would need to be made.

The utilization of coaching may involve specific areas where coaches focus on predetermined issues, or it may involve nonspecific areas, where the coach looks for areas of improvement in teacher instruction. Providing individualized coaching to the teacher is an essential component in the model and it is necessary to tailor the mentoring to the individual teacher's needs.

COACHING BENEFITS

The following studies provide evidence for the benefits of coaching for both preservice and practicing teachers.

Bowman and McCormick (2000) found that coaching increased preservice teachers' clarity of instruction, pedagogical reasoning, and action skills. During the preservice teacher field experience, thirty-two participants were randomly assigned to a group that employed coaching dyads or to a group that experienced a traditional supervision approach.

The coaching dyads were a *reciprocal* type of coaching experience between preservice teachers. The teacher dyads observed and informally evaluated each other, exchanged constructive feedback, and collaboratively engaged in critical dialogue. Open-ended questions from an attitude scale revealed that both the coached and traditional group were satisfied with the overall experience; however, content analysis indicated the coaching participants had a greater number of favorable comments about the field experience as compared to the traditional participants.

In a study by Showers (1982) to determine the effect of coaching on the transfer of training, seventeen middle school and junior high teachers were trained in three models of teaching (Bruner's Concept Attainment, Taba's Inductive Thinking, and Gordon's Synectics). All teachers attended twenty-one hours of initial skills training on the teaching models. At the conclusion of the initial training, half of the teachers were randomly assigned to receive the *coaching* treatment while the remaining teachers were observed but not coached.

The findings revealed that coaching was a statistically significant predictor of the teachers' ability to transfer training and that many of the non-coached group discontinued use of the new teaching models after the initial training. In another study by Showers (1984), coaching was found to significantly increase the ability of middle and junior high school teachers to transfer new models of teaching into their daily instruction. An additional finding was the positive effect on student learning.

COACHING AND THE BRAIN

In recent years, coaching has increasingly been identified as a way to strengthen neuropathways. David Rock's (2006) research in the field of neuroscience indicates that new wiring can be created that provides connections with new choices for thinking and behavior.

Betz (2015) suggests three ways in which coaching helps to integrate the brain. First, coaching helps clients (teachers, candidates, colleagues, etc.) move from a reactive tendency to a more creative and productive experience. In other words, coaching helps connect with more innovative solutions. Second, coaching assists the individual being coached to make deep, lasting changes according to what is meaningful, valued, and purposeful. Third, coaching helps individuals integrate the brain hemispheres, thus implementing projects that are desired.

PURPOSE AND ORGANIZATION OF THE BOOK

With the research findings on the effectiveness of coaching in mind, the purpose of this book is to provide educators, teacher preparation programs, and professional development providers a resource to assist them in using coaching to improve teacher practices across all content areas and grade levels.

Through our experiences as classroom teachers, instructional coaches, and teacher educators and researchers, we hope that educators will be able to use this book when seeking to improve teacher preparation programs and to provide quality professional development. All of the authors are experienced teachers, teacher educators, administrators, and/or instructional coaches.

Each chapter includes an overview, a detailed discussion, and practical applications of coaching. Each chapter concludes with a summary and questions for reflection.

The book is organized into three sections. Section I introduces coaching as an educational practice, describes the skills needed for coaching, and emphasizes the necessity of relatedness in coaching dyads.

Section II discusses how coaching can be used in teacher preparation programs. At our university, teacher candidates are coached by their faculty supervisor, peers, and supervising teacher during practicum or internship experiences. Coaching is used to help teacher candidates develop self-efficacy, improve instructional practices, and increase their professionalism. The chapters describe how coaching occurs using a face-to-face traditional format or through a bug in the ear virtual format.

Finally, section III focuses on providing professional development to practicing teachers using coaching. Coaching descriptions include both face-to-face and virtual formats as well as personal accounts of coaching novice teachers and coaching teachers in specific content areas.

It is our hope that this book will be a valuable resource to you, our readers, and that you will be able to take what we have learned about coaching and apply it to your specific situation to improve education for all children. Finally, we wish to thank our esteemed and very busy colleagues who diligently provided their expertise, knowledge, and personal experiences in writing their chapters. This book would not have been possible without their contributions.

Section I

Instructional Coaching as an Educational Practice

In this first section, readers will be introduced to instructional coaching as an educational practice. Beginning with the first chapter, those skills that set coaching apart from other instructional roles will be examined. Coaching skills applied in a virtual setting will conclude the chapter. Chapter 2 introduces readers to a unique application of coaching skills. By focusing on coaching for affective development, this chapter hones in on the importance of relatedness as a means of creating a positive climate and culture in which students and/or teachers feel safe as they are achieving academically and applying new instructional skills.

Chapter One

Essential Coaching Skills

Patty Kohler-Evans, EdD,
University of Central Arkansas

Effective coaching focused at the classroom level, with an emphasis on the implementation of research-based instructional strategies for all students, has great potential for generating student gains. The case for instructional coaching has been previously stated; however, it is critical that the reader have a deeper understanding of the essential elements that set coaching apart from other instructional roles. By focusing on and developing these essential skills, an instructional coach, whether he or she is a colleague, supervisor, university professor, or other professional, can impact classroom instruction in ways unimagined.

Whether the relationship is carried out face-to-face, via phone, through bug in the ear, or other format, the essential coaching skills discussed in this chapter must be present in order for the coaching relationship to be effective. Coaching is most powerful when the specific skills of committed listening, paraphrasing, presuming positive intent, asking powerful questions, and providing reflective feedback are used within a framework of a genuine partnership philosophy.

This chapter will delve into each of these skills and how they contribute to improving outcomes for all students. Although the essential coaching skills are interdependent, they will be discussed singly, and the relationships between and among the skills will be explored as each one is highlighted. At the end of the chapter is a section on the unique considerations regarding the application of coaching skills in a virtual setting.

COMMITTED LISTENING

In *Taking the Lead*, Killion and Harrison (2006) reflect on the myriad roles that coaches fulfill in public school classrooms. From resource provider to curriculum specialist, learning facilitator, or catalyst for change, no role is more important than that of committed listener.

One of the first individuals to focus widespread light on the importance of listening was Stephen Covey (1989), with his fifth habit, *seek first to understand, then to be understood* (p. 53). It becomes obvious when examining the role of coach that Covey is suggesting that sharing an incredible strategy or even offering a new behavioral program is best received when the person to whom the strategy or program is being offered has been heard.

Hearing implies more than using one's ears to process sound; in this context, hearing means the listener has deeply understood the speaker. As Covey so aptly states, "Most people don't listen with the intent to understand; they listen with the intent to reply" (p. 239).

Knight's (2007) research in innovation implementation revealed that teachers who were interviewed about professional development indicated that they frequently felt undervalued as educators and they were often told what to do without being consulted. An effective coach must listen. As the old adage *people don't care what you know until they know you care* suggests, unless one knows he or she is cared about (listened to), it does not matter what the message is.

The consequences of failing to fully listen can be dire. A failure to be heard can result in frustration, anger, disregard, and even indifference on the part of the speaker while leading to disengagement and a failure to implement even the most promising or research-validated methods.

Listening is the "foundational skill for all communication skill" according to Kee et al. (2010). Dennis Sparks (2006), former director of the National Staff Development Council, suggests that "committed listening transforms relationships and deepens learning" (p. 52). The International Coaching Federation (ICF) identifies active listening as a core competency (http://www.coachfederation.org/credential/landing.cfm?ItemNumber=2206) and a key strategy in communicating effectively with another person in a coaching relationship (ICF, n.d.).

In his classic work on relationships, Gottman (2001) discusses listening as an essential emotional communication skill, offering that listening can help make relations stronger by repairing communication problems. Madelyn Burley-Allen (1995) developed a series of self-assessments for the aspiring better listener that help by targeting communication knowledge and attitudes.

These assessments were designed to provide a spotlight on the critical component of quality, committed listening, by highlighting such elements as listening to what one wants to hear instead of what the speaker is saying and giving the appearance of listening when one is not actually focused on the speaker. The self-assessments can provide a springboard from which to grow as a listener.

In summary, a committed listener exhibits several behaviors including concentrating on what the speaker is saying, setting aside judgment, solution finding, or personal stories during the discourse, allowing the speaker to complete his or her thoughts before speaking, listening for the whole message (verbal and nonverbal), recognizing that words don't necessarily mean the same to everyone, honoring another's views even when different from one's own, and refraining from providing advice. In essence, listening is being fully present with another human being. Any coach who seeks to impact lasting positive change must start by being a committed listener.

PARAPHRASING

Susan Scott (2002) uses the phrase "the conversation is the relationship" (p. 5) to emphasize the incredible importance of coaching conversations. Scott urges coaches to "use paraphrasing and perception checks; don't be satisfied with what's on the surface" (p. 157). Paraphrasing is the second essential coaching skill and, like listening, it can greatly enhance or impede the conversation. Paraphrasing is closely linked to listening and can be described as the evidence that committed listening has actually taken place.

According to the Oxford Dictionary, paraphrase means to "express the meaning of the speaker using different words, especially to achieve greater clarity." A closer examination of the definition reveals that the essence is not in simply using different words, but, more importantly, in using words to achieve greater clarity.

It should become immediately clear that there is an incredible relationship between listening and paraphrasing. Without committed listening, it is virtually impossible to gain a clearer understanding and reflect that understanding in the words that are spoken back to the speaker.

Returning to Stephen Covey's fifth habit, *seek first to understand, then to be understood*, an essential element of understanding means checking with the speaker through use of a powerful paraphrase, one that in essence says, "This is what I heard; is this what you meant to say?"

The art of paraphrasing can be tricky. Delving more deeply into Scott's statement about diving "below the surface," paraphrasing is the perfect skill to use when exploring the speaker's spoken as well as unspoken words. The experienced coach listens, watches, observes, and then summarizes both what is observed and what is not observed. A quality paraphrase is crisp and to the point, yet captures the essence of the speaker's message.

Principles of quality paraphrasing include being fully attentive by setting aside competing distractors or barriers, listening with the intent to understand, capturing the essence of the message, reflecting on the essence of voice tone and gestures, and paraphrasing before asking questions.

The effective coach must remember that paraphrasing should send powerful messages: I am listening, I care, and I understand you. It is not difficult to see how paraphrasing complements the skill of committed listening.

PRESUMING POSITIVE INTENT

Presuming positive intent refers to the coach's beliefs and thoughts about what the speaker is saying. This skill begins with a presupposition, which is anything that a native speaker of a language knows is part of the deeper meaning of a sequence of the language. The reader is invited to think about the presuppositions we make every day.

We think we know. In fact, we say, "I know . . ." We just know. We make judgments all the time, and our language reflects that. Judgment is a force that helps us make sense of the world, yet our judgments, left unexamined, can leave us focused on what is wrong in the world and in ourselves as well as others.

One's language has the ability to shape thoughts, feelings, and experiences, and a skilled coach uses language to its full positive potential by becoming aware of his or her habitual ways of speaking. More importantly, attentive coaches are fully aware of the messages they send to others, especially the person being coached. If a coach is deeply attentive to his or her own presuppositions and chooses words with care, the thinking and feeling of the individual being coached can be positively impacted, thus resulting in improved outcomes for the students placed in his or her care.

Three key behaviors have been identified by the authors of *Powerful Coaching* (Coaching for Results Global, 2013), an accredited coach training program: (1) the listener presumes the speaker has positive intentions in all actions and behaviors; (2) the listener presumes the speaker has previously thought, said, or done what the speaker is asking about, and the listener's language reflects this; and (3) the listener uses positive presuppositions in his or her own language to "demonstrate genuine belief in the positive thinking and actions of the speaker" (p. 11).

Presuming positive intent, in essence, means that as a coach, all notions of judgment are placed aside, and the coach believes in the positive intent of the speaker. Although sometimes difficult to do, the presumption of positive intent can greatly enhance an effective coaching relationship and open the door to assisting the person being coached to seek solutions that can have a positive and lasting impact on student performance.

ASKING POWERFUL QUESTIONS

We have all had that moment when a friend, loved one, or even colleague has asked us a question that left us stunned and silent for a moment, the question that made us take a step into ourselves and ponder. These packed yet simple questions sometimes leave us with a totally different perspective or even result in paradigm shift. They can be as simple as, "What did you mean by that?" or the famous Dr. Phil question, "How did that work for you?" Powerful questions are those that "lead to discovery, insight, and commitment to action" (Kee et al., 2010). Asking powerful questions is the next essential coaching skill that will be explored.

According to Maxwell (2008), the most meaningful mentoring (coaching) moments are based on carefully designed questions. Bearwald (2011) suggests that effective coaching thrives on questioning and listening rather than quick fixes. Coaches should ask specific types of questions: those that target essential issues and behavior, those that are precise and lead to greater clarity, questions that generate specific, relevant information, those that explore values, and those that connect past, present, and future (Bearwald, 2011).

Questions can be essential or nonessential, according to McTighe and Wiggins (2013). These authors discuss the art of questioning within the context of the teacher–student relationship, however, quality questions within a coaching relationship possess the same basic characteristics.

First, high-quality questions are open ended. Stephen Barkley (2005) discusses the importance of asking open-ended questions when working with teachers or teacher candidates, indicating that a "closed-ended question controls the direction of communication," while "in the open-ended question, the answer controls the direction" (p. 56).

High-quality questions are thought provoking, intellectually engaging, and call for higher-order thinking. A skilled coach is proficient in asking questions that elicit a coachee's "creativity, values, or personalized information" (Barkley, 2005, p. 109). According to McTighe and Wiggins (2013), quality questions also point toward "important transferable ideas," raise "additional questions," require "support and justification," and recur "over time" (p. 3). In essence, the questions that an intuitive and attentive coach asks are deeply provocative. Borrowing the words of Wiggins and McTighe (2005), these questions "push us to the heart—the essence" (p. 107).

Within a coaching context, sometimes the coach is not the only individual who is asking questions. Ronald Bearwald (2011) warns that coaches should avoid responding to the mentee's questions when the purpose of the question is to look for answers. According to Bearwald, "Offering answers to every question can lead to a dysfunctional dance that short-circuits higher-level thinking" (p. 74). Bearwald comments, "When a mentor (coach) provides a solution or makes a decision for a mentee, the mentor unwittingly inhibits the reflection needed to identify desirable courses of action" (p. 74).

Undoubtedly, questioning effectively is a skill that needs careful cultivation. In short, questions can help teachers and candidates reflect, explore, examine, analyze, and dig deeper into their practices and use of instructional or behavioral strategies. There is no substitute for a powerful question, especially when the coach adds committed listening, paraphrasing, and the presumption of positive intent to the mix.

PROVIDING REFLECTIVE FEEDBACK

Providing reflective feedback is another critical skill that effective coaches utilize when working with teachers. In order for feedback to be received, a trusting relationship must be established between the coach and the one being coached. Providing feedback may sound simple on the surface, yet like other coaching skills, it is difficult to do in such a way that feedback is received as nonjudgmental as well as evaluation free.

Traditionally, feedback has usually been given as judgment, a personal observation, inference, some type of data, or questions. Feedback is essential if our commitment as coaches is to promote another's learning. In this section, considerations regarding the effective provision of reflective feedback will be explored.

Several suggestions for providing feedback effectively have been identified by Kee et al. (2010). Specifically, recommendations are be specific, be generous, ask permission before providing feedback, remember the goal is self-directed learning, and avoid negative feedback. As professional and licensed coaches, these authors also remind aspiring coaches to consider that the art of giving effective feedback takes thought and practice. Finally, feedback is not the only answer to improving student success; it is but one of many answers.

When coaches are engaged in the process of providing reflective feedback, it is imperative that a partnership perspective is utilized. Jim Knight's (2007) partnership principles may apply with feedback more so than with any other of the coaching skills. *Equality* implies that both coach and individual being coached are co-equals, with thoughts and beliefs held to be equally valuable. *Choice* means that a teacher's choice is "implicit in every communicative act" (p. 24), and *voice* suggests that both partners have opportunities to express their points of view.

Dialogue means that coaches listen more than they tell. *Reflection* suggests that the person being coached is able to make sense of whatever the coach is proposing, and nowhere is this as important as in giving feedback; true partners do not dictate what is to be believed. Finally, *praxis* implies that teachers may reconstruct and use content in whatever way they consider most useful. The coach's presumption of positive intent, his or her full presence as a listener, the posing of provocative questions, and use of clear paraphrasing all come together beautifully with partnership principles when feedback is effectively provided.

COACHING IN A VIRTUAL SETTING

As coaches are increasingly utilizing technology and distance learning methods to impact change through coaching, a few comments about virtual coaching seem worthy of mention here. The coaching relationship, especially when conducted virtually, should build on several underlying qualities for both participants in the relationship: a willingness to change, a trusting relationship, a high level of initiative, and a personal and organizational commitment to the workplace (Blackman, 2010).

Jude Tavanyar (2014) suggests that coaches attend to virtual etiquette by setting norms for engagement in a virtual setting while creating a safe space for "skillful, free-flowing exploratory dialogue" (p. 9). Tavanyar identifies emotional connection as essential, especially when talking in cyberspace. Emotional connection can begin with a simple check in or inquiry about the state of being of the person being coached. In addition, Tavanyar emphasizes the need for listening in such a way that it becomes absolutely obvious that the coach is fully present. Using nudge questions such as "Yes?" "And so . . . ?" and "And then . . . ?" can emphasize presence.

Vocal presence is also important, and here the listener/coach needs to show connection, warmth, and concern through use of tone and pace. Finally, the coach should consider his or her visual presence so that the person being coached knows what the coach looks like, especially if a webcam is not being used. This can be done by providing photos as visually presented welcoming information.

A skilled coach will seek to connect with those being coached no matter what the format, however, noting some virtual considerations has the potential to deepen the level of trust and intimacy between the coach and the coached. By considering these recommendations, the virtual coaching experience can be greatly enhanced.

SUMMARY

Coaching provides amazing opportunities to cultivate and build foundational and life-changing relationships with the potential to impact student success in unimagined ways. Coaching distinguishes itself from other academic roles in several critical ways. Skilled coaches must be fully committed listeners, making the promise to be here, nowhere else, and to listen deeply for what is being said as well as what is left unsaid. Paired with committed listening, a coach affirms the speaker has been heard through powerfully stated paraphrases that, in essence, say to the speaker, "I am seeking to fully understand you."

In addition to listening and paraphrasing, a coach presumes the speaker has noble purposes by presuming positive intent. The speaker may or may not know how to effectively implement strategies, methods, or plans with students in his or her care, but his or her intent stands strong.

A coach asks precise, crisp questions designed to provoke deeper understanding and generate high-quality solutions. Finally, a coach, through all interactions, provides reflective feedback by gently and firmly holding a mirror to the speaker, always checking to make sure to fully *reflect* the speaker's words, intentions, emotions, and beliefs.

QUESTIONS FOR REFLECTION

In order to develop your skills as a coach, please consider these questions for reflection.

1. As you think about the essential coaching skills, which ones are strengths for you? Which ones provide challenges?
2. How do you want to "show up" as a coach?
3. In what ways do you honor the speaker through your committed listening?
4. How do you paraphrase both the content and emotions of the speaker?
5. How do you demonstrate genuine belief in the positive thinking and actions of the speaker?
6. In what ways do you pose powerful questions to challenge the speaker to "push to the heart—the essence?"
7. How do you infuse care, respect, and honesty into your reflective feedback?
8. What commitments are you willing to make in order to become a highly effective coach?

Chapter Two

Coaching for Affective Development

Candice Dowd Barnes, EdD, University of Central Arkansas

Coaching for affective development can be a deeply personal and relational endeavor that can affect the genuineness of the interactions among educators, students, and others. It involves the engagement of a relationship-focused approach. It operationalizes emotions. It also connects emotion and cognition to increase motivation and learning. The obvious next questions are:

- What is coaching for affective development?
- How do we coach for affective development?
- Why is this type of coaching important to the instructional process?

This chapter will focus on the importance of developing a sense of trust, credibility, and a thinking partnership when coaching others to develop their affective domain to find a measure of success in the classroom. This chapter will also provide examples and a *dress rehearsal*—a scenario to further explain and offer essentials to engage in affective development coaching. Included at the end of the dress rehearsal are questions for reflection.

DEFINING COACHING FOR AFFECTIVE DEVELOPMENT

Coaching for affective development draws upon feelings, cognition, and behavior—the subcomponents of emotion. When coaching for affective development one must also consider attitudes, values, and beliefs. Therefore, coaching for affective development addresses how one's personality traits, characteristics, dispositions, emotions, thoughts, physiology, and value system drive how you interact and engage with others genuinely. Coaching for affective development also encompasses how we connect to others' emotions, our ability to regulate our emotions and interactions, and how we address the elements of relatedness.

According to Parker, Barnes, and Kohler-Evans (2016), there are five key elements of relatedness. Those elements are relationship, routines, respect, responsiveness, and rapport. Each element is equally important to how the culture and climate of the classroom is impacted. However, coaching for affective development is most closely aligned to developing rapport, respect, and being responsive to the needs of the person being coached, in this context the teacher or teacher candidate.

Coaching teachers to address how their affective domain influences the classroom culture and climate can be complex. It is through a relationship-centered approach, however, that coaches and teachers can operationalize their affective domains to create a context in which the teacher feels safe, connected, and valued. This is similar to how teachers must create a classroom context in which their students feel valued and emotionally safe.

The relationship-centered approach satisfies the emotional needs and supports a framework for learning to occur. This approach values the students' knowledge and experiences and does not lower standards in an effort to create false satisfaction for the student or teacher. It is generally based on the rapport that is created, a sense of self-concept, and an awareness of efficacy.

Consider what is commonly understood in neuroscience. There is a direct connection to the emotional and cognitive domains. When students feel emotionally safe, and their contributions to the culture and climate of the classroom are valued, they are more likely to engage in learning (Rogers and Renard, 1999). When the student places a high value on the learning, the meaning of that learning is deepened and more satisfying.

It is more likely than not that the student will retain more content leading to greater mastery and proficiency. This same relationship-centered approach when applied allows the teachers to effect change in their classrooms positively. This same concept holds true for coaches and teachers, especially when coaching for affective development.

When teachers are developing a trusting, credible, thinking partnership with their coach, there is a connection between the emotional and cognitive domains. The teacher feels a certain level of emotional safety allowing him or her to engage in constructive conversations that will impact how he or she, the teacher, will influence the learning environment and students. A supportive safety net allows the teacher to communicate openly and think offensively with his or her coach.

This connection also creates a space in which the coach and the teacher seek the best practices to ensure learning occurs in an academically safe environment. Furthermore, trusting, credible, thinking partnerships are supported by the underlying relatedness principles: rapport, responsiveness, and respect.

These underlying principles, rapport, respect, and responsiveness, build the foundation for in-depth and highly effective coaching to occur and a thinking partnership to develop. These principles create a space for *real* coaching that does not rely on fix-it techniques. Rapport, respect, and responsiveness create a space for the coach to be the facilitator of deep thinking, new perspectives, new ideas, and differentiated approaches to meet the needs of all learners. The teacher can then become the primary thinker or problem solver, forfeiting the dependency on the coach's expertise and advice.

Let us continue to explore the connection between the underlying relatedness principles and the importance of trust, credibility, and deep thinking to create an effective thinking partnership. The next section will guide the reader through five elements designed to grow a thinking partnership in which rapport, respect, and responsiveness are realized.

Near the end of this chapter is a dress rehearsal related to those underlying principles and the importance of creating a thinking partnership. The dress rehearsal or short scenario provides an opportunity to reflect and engage the mind, body, and spirit to coach for affective development and classroom change.

GROWING A THINKING PARTNERSHIP

Developing rapport, respect, and responding to the needs of the teacher can be a delicate balance of patience and understanding. There is an adage that trust is easy to lose and hard to gain. This is especially true when coaching practicing professionals. The same adage similarly applies to developing rapport and respect in particular.

Rapport can be lost easily if not cultivated consistently. Respect is gained when trust is established. Responsiveness is inflated by a sense of care and consideration. Furthermore, this delicate balance can be disrupted or can quickly nosedive into disrepair when dominated by poorly handled emotional functioning.

Initially and intrinsically, most teachers will be guarded. Their administrators may have informed them of an issue that negatively affects their teaching. Perhaps they received an undesirable performance evaluation. They may even be intimidated by the coach's knowledge and expertise driving them to perform a dog and pony show. It is the job of the coach to create a context for trust to develop—to grow and undergird the thinking partnership.

Covey's (1989) concept of first seek to understand is essential when developing this sense of trust so that rapport can flourish. Building on that concept are five essentials to develop rapport and trust, preserve credibility, and respond to the needs of the teacher. These essentials promote the growth of the teacher's affective development that will influence his or her instructional and teaching effectiveness.

1. *Know the teacher, both personally and professionally.* Make him or her feel comfortable to open up. For some this might be a fast process. For others, it may happen at a much slower rate. Start with the basic conversational question. Then pivot to more in-depth questions and conversations that will paint a more detailed picture of his or her humanity.

Exploring the teacher's humanity is key. It aids one in learning how the teacher contributes to the successes and failures that occur within the classroom. It also allows the coach to gain greater insight or awareness into how this person's emotional components are developed. For example, what classroom management strategies is the teacher using to address behavior and routines? What types of hobbies does the teacher have, and how does he or she integrate those hobbies into his or her respective classrooms? What brings contentment, joy, frustration, or euphoria into his or her life? Learning more about his or her personal and professional triumphs and struggles signals to the teacher that the coach cares and is genuinely interested in his or her welfare, and not just improving the quality of his or her teaching.

2. *Encourage the teacher to share what he or she values and believes about learning, the students, the classroom, school, or community culture, etc.* This again will give you greater insight into how one might bolster the teacher's successes. Remember the relationship-centered approach is the driving force behind coaching for affective development aptitude.

Therefore, coaching for affective development, in this context, is predicated on learning more about how the teacher makes meaning of his or her work and learning environment. For example, if the teacher speaks disparagingly about his or her students' life circumstances, this may provide greater understanding of the value that teacher places on the students' abilities, skills, and motivation to learn.

If a teacher rejects connecting with students who are emotionally or socially challenged, students whose school experiences have caused grave consequences to their self-esteem and motivation for learning, or students with complex emotional functioning, it may help discern the level to which the teacher is committed to ensuring student achievement and success. Learning what the teacher values will certainly affect the rapport and level of trust between the coach and teacher. It may also influence the level of credibility and responsiveness between the two.

Likewise, if the teacher shares stories of triumph or graceful failures or the teacher can discuss with pleasure and pain facts and stories about the community, the family, and the school, it provides insight into his or her emotional functioning—the discernment of how emotion is understood, managed, regulated, and expressed. In these instances the coach can create a space to engage the teacher in learning outcomes, meaningful strategies, and deep thinking to grow the partnership to achieve the highest expectations.

3. *Learn how his or her personality characteristics influence his or her practices, productivity, and motivation.* Using a tool like the Personality Package, for example, helps to unpack the layers to one's personality that will undoubtedly influence the classroom culture and climate (Parker, Barnes, and Kohler-Evans, 2016). It is critical to explore how one's traits, characteristics, and dispositions are intraconnected and displayed when working with an individual student and/or groups of students.

Addressing these traits and characteristics speaks directly to the way in which one responds appropriately and authentically to classroom and school situations. As the coach, avoid making assumptions based on your impression and perception of the teacher's personality characteristics or your prior experiences with other teachers who might share similar outward characteristics. The following scenario illustrates how rapport is developed once assumptions on personality characteristics are addressed.

Hannah's students are predominately minority students who live in a low-income neighborhood in which many families have felt the pain of violence, gangs, and drug activity. Most of their experiences and interactions with white people are typically in a social service or law enforcement context. They walk into her classroom for the first time. They see her as a young, white, female teacher. Their prior experiences and interactions cause them to place an unfair judgment on who Hannah is genuinely.

They may automatically assume or presume based on their impression, perceptions, and experiences that she will be quiet, reserved, and a pushover. On the other hand, they may assume that she will be afraid, intrusive, or untrustworthy. It may be difficult for them to connect with her based on those impressions and perceptions.

After a couple of weeks of Hannah working to develop rapport with her students, after a few conversations, the students learned that Hannah grew up in a poor, rural community where she experienced many of the same social ills associated with violence and drug activity. They also learned that she grew up listening to old-school hip-hop and is a huge fan of the group Public Enemy.

Her students are shocked when Hannah accurately and authentically recites lyrics from TuPac and Public Enemy. They learned that she writes poetry, plays the guitar, and is a math whiz. The students' perceptions change of who Hannah is because she has presented herself genuinely. From that point, rapport grows. Apply a similar scenario to a teacher and coach.

When Hannah meets her coach for the first time, she sees him as a middle-aged, African American, male educator. She automatically assumes or presumes that he will be able to help her manage the misbehaviors of her African American male students. She quickly learns that he is a math and science specialist who also struggled with classroom management and misbehavior. She learns that his upbringing is quite dissimilar to his students'. She becomes acutely aware that her life experiences intersect with her students' far more than his do.

He shares how rapport was a real issue with his African American male students and that some of his students referred to him as a square. Still, he offers some stories of triumph and struggle and strategies he used that might help her with classroom management. Hannah's perception of him and his coaching prowess changes and rapport begins to develop because he is no longer bound by her perceptions of who she wants him to be, but her perception is a reflection of who he is genuinely.

Learning the personality characteristics and how those characteristics are perceived by self and others help you move from the impression to perception, to reflection, and then practice and perform. Like Rome, rapport and respect are not built in a day. It will take time, and in some cases, great effort to create a relationship-centered context to effectively coach for affective development.

When coaching for affective development, acknowledging how the teacher is presenting him- or herself to students is crucial. It affects the classroom instruction, culture, and climate. When teachers genuinely present who they are in the classroom, change is inevitable. It allows one to foster positive emotions that can create a context for learning to occur. Coaches, then, should find tools to help teachers identify and operationalize their personalities, dispositions, and motivations into practices that support successful learning and satisfy social-emotional outcomes.

4. *Honor their standing, their position.* Be up front and specific about the purpose and the role of the coach in context. Give the information needed, allowing the teacher to formalize his or her opinions and place a value on the time spent coaching. Use and define terms and phrases like *constructive feedback*, *coaching conversations*, and *focused feedback*. These phrases signify that you are responding to his or her needs in a caring, authentic manner designed to maintain high standards and deflate lowering standards to produce artificial feelings of success.

Coach with intentionality so that when unintended outcomes arise, trust is maintained through the rapport that has been developed. Hard conversations are inevitable. Honoring who he or she is in his or her own classroom and the experiences he or she brings can continue to support the relationship. Honor the teacher's status by building on a learning context, not a judgmental or evaluative approach (Kee et al., 2010). Respect them as a member in the thinking partnership, not just the receiver of good advice.

5. *Discuss the areas the teacher desires to enhance.* Notice the use of the word *enhance* and not *improve*. Enhance implies positive thinking, a positive outlook. Improve usually implies negative or ineffective practices. However

true this may be, building rapport to cultivate trust is easier when built from offensive thinking and not defensive thinking. As the coach, you want the teacher to be motivated to think, learn, and trust. Therefore, evidence of success and progress shows his or her work toward mastery. Help the teacher identify and reflect upon the areas where he or she has been successful and build upon those successes, large and small.

DRESS REHEARSAL

Let us continue to follow Hannah's story and reflect on how the five essentials are used effectively to build a thinking partnership based on rapport, respect, and responsiveness to the needs of the teacher. At the end of the dress rehearsal are questions to engage one's thinking about how coaching practices affect the teacher's affective development and promote classroom change.

Initially Hannah was hesitant to share her thoughts about what she could do to change the misbehavior in her classroom. Most of her students responded well to her opening up about her musical influences, poetry, and such. A few of her students who also shared similar interests asked if they could take some of her poetry to create a rap song. She was thrilled and honored. Still, Hannah was challenged by a few of her students with whom she just could not connect, no matter what she tried. Yet she was not going to give up.

When Mr. Lymon was assigned to Hannah as her coach, he made a point to schedule a sacred time each day to meet with her. He wanted to get to know a little about her, what she thought about her students, where they struggled, where they were successful, and what she wanted to accomplish from their coaching time. Hannah felt empowered, as she did not know what to expect and was unsure of how they would interact and connect. She was happy that Mr. Lymon did not judge or devalue her role in the classroom, her knowledge, or her lack of experience in some areas. In fact, Mr. Lymon celebrated where she was successful and gave her a few ideas of how to build upon those successes.

After a couple of weeks of getting to know Mr. Lymon, she felt a bit more confident to speak up about a radical idea for how she might be able to build a bridge to those disconnected, misbehaving students. She ran into him in the hallway and told him that she had something she wanted discuss, but was not sure if it would be appropriate for her class and needed some advice. Hannah and Mr. Lymon met during their sacred time to talk through her idea.

Based on previous conversations with Hannah and what he knew about her personality already, he was certain that whatever this idea was would probably involve music, math, or both. Indeed, he was right. Her idea was innovative and creative. He asked lots of thinking questions to help her create a plan to engage all of her students in a music appreciation project that included an invitation to the students' favorite local hip-hop artist.

SUMMARY

Coaching for affective development is an ongoing process. It is based on several factors, including the constant cultivation of rapport, maintaining trust, developing a quality relationship, understanding first before being understood, a reliance on one's intrinsic motivation to learn, deep thinking, and an emotionally safe environment to express sentiment, concerns, and ask questions.

Coaching is about creating a relationship-focused or relationship-centered context that is meaningful for the teacher—an environment in which learning occurs for the coach, the teacher, and the student. When the teacher is comfortable and confident enough to foster a thinking partnership with his or her coach, the teacher's emotional functioning and intraconnectedness grows and he or she can often find greater contentment in his or her work.

QUESTIONS FOR REFLECTION

1. How did Mr. Lymon and Hannah foster a sense of rapport, respect, and responsiveness in the scenario? What specific evidence supports the essential elements of coaching for affective development?
2. At what point did trust and credibility factor into the interactions between Hannah and Mr. Lymon?
3. What strategies and approaches are you currently implementing to grow a thinking partnership with your teacher or teacher candidate? What types of thinking questions do you pose that respond to his or her needs without giving him or her fix-it techniques?
4. How would you evaluate the rapport you have with him or her, and is the level of trust you have built with him or her sustainable?

Section II

Coaching Teacher Candidates

Section II offers insights to coaching teacher candidates. The first chapter in this section, chapter 3, describes today's traditional and nontraditional teacher candidates, the roles and responsibilities of mentor/coaches, and how this relationship benefits both candidates and coaches. Chapter 4 describes a triad of instructional coaching with the teacher candidate being coached by university instructors, school supervising teachers, and cohort peers. This chapter is focused on math and science teachers but is applicable to any and all content areas. The section concludes with a description of how one university utilizes virtual technology for observation and coaching in teacher candidates' culminating internship course. The university found that this type of supervision removes the barrier of distance and allows for more frequent coaching interactions.

Chapter Three

LEAP into Mentoring Teacher Candidates

Nancy P. Gallavan, PhD,
University of Central Arkansas

> No significant learning occurs without a significant relationship.
> —James Comer (2004)

Most educator preparation programs are framed by standards and regulations by which teacher educators design and deliver their programs and policies (Council for the Accreditation of Educator Preparation [CAEP], 2015). Teacher educators are continually seeking ways to improve teacher candidate preparation and pedagogical practices and to increase teacher candidate retention in their programs and as career professionals. Concomitantly, teacher candidates are navigating higher education to fulfill their aspirations for becoming P–12 classroom teachers much like the classroom teachers with whom they interacted while in elementary, middle, and high school.

Candidates' goals focus on replicating the teaching, learning, and schooling experiences by establishing a similar sense of place that brought them success and satisfaction in their youth. However, as teacher candidates embark on their travels in higher education, they encounter challenges and changes that impact both their journeys inward and their journeys outward (Conway and Clark, 2003).

Given that many candidates are becoming young adults with ever-expanding responsibilities, entering higher education as first-generation university students, seeking careers new to their families and friends, and pursuing complex professional careers that are constantly expanded and modified, teacher educators are exploring avenues and advantages for mentoring and coaching their teacher candidates. Many candidates benefit from the guidance and support of mentors: trusted advisers who possess insight and inspiration associated with efficacy and agency shared in small-group and/or one-on-one environments.

Mentors coach candidates with sundry knowledge, skills, and dispositions related to the dynamics of the profession: their personal growth, professional development, pedagogical expertise, and political astuteness that contribute to candidates' self-efficacy and sense of agency, two desired qualities of career educators (Gallavan, 2016). This chapter describes today's teacher candidates, the roles and responsibilities of mentor/coaches, the LEAP approach for mentoring/coaching candidates, and the benefits for both candidates and coaches.

TODAY'S TEACHER CANDIDATES

Based on their university student status and their age ranges, today's teacher candidates can be sorted into one of three groups: (1) undergraduate students approximately eighteen to twenty-two years of age, in this chapter referenced as undergraduate teacher candidate basic (UTCB); (2) undergraduate students older than approximately twenty-two years of age, referenced as undergraduate teacher candidate multifaceted (UTCM); and (3) graduate students older than approximately twenty-two years of age, referenced as graduate teacher candidate multifaceted (GTCM).

The UTCB tends to have entered the university directly from high school or to have transferred from a community college. The UTCM tends to have followed similar paths to the UTCB and requires additional time to complete the degree due to university major changes, family or financial obligations, other opportunities, etc.

The GTCM tends to have earned a university degree in an academic area other than education and has decided to become a P–12 teacher. Frequently the GTCM is considered a career changer; the GTCM has pursued another career successfully, started a family, and has become an established member of the community. Returning to higher education is often accompanied by concerns for the candidate, the candidate's family, the candidate's employment, and, frequently, the candidate's ability to accommodate the technological advances associated with higher education.

In general, teacher candidates across all three groups are enrolled in educator preparation programs framed by similar accepted standards and academic expectations aligned with national accreditation associations and state department of education licensure regulations. Although the program organization and course delivery within each educator preparation program may differ across the United States, many teacher educators are increasing their awareness of and their endeavors to mentor or coach their candidates in order to increase candidates' engagement and achievement (self-efficacy) while in the program coupled with enhancing candidates' professionalism and retention (agency) throughout their careers (Darling-Hammond, 2010; Zeichner, 2010).

As the research related to the purposes and values of mentoring or coaching teacher candidates becomes more refined and offers teacher educators insights to advance their candidates' and their own passions and practices, teacher educators must remember to contextualize their guidance and support based on the stages and ages of their teacher candidates.

MENTORING AND COACHING

The word *mentor* is taken from *The Odyssey* authored by Homer (800 BCE). In *The Odyssey*, Mentor, a close friend of Odysseus, was entrusted with the education of his son, Telemachus. As Telemachus embarked on his lifelong journey, he gained courage, strength, and wisdom based on Mentor's guidance and support integrated with reliance and respect (Emory University, n.d.). Over time, the word *mentor* has evolved to mean trusted friend, advisor, teacher, wise person, and so forth. Much like Telemachus, today's teacher candidates are embarking on their lifelong journeys, hopefully benefiting through their relationships with mentors.

Today the word *mentor*, for many people, including educators, also means coach. Although coaching and mentoring are closely aligned, the Association for Talent Development (ATD) differentiates coaching from mentoring in that coaching manifests as a more formal and organized relationship focused on improvements to resolve immediate issues or specific concerns (ATD, n.d.). Coaching educators, that is, teacher candidates, classroom teachers, and teacher educators, involves peer-to-peer conversations that provide objective feedback related to the recipient's strengths and weaknesses on issues chosen together by the coach and recipient.

Led by the coach, conversations encourage both the coach and the recipient to ask questions, explore answers, and set goals. Typically the coach does not evaluate the recipient yet encourages the recipient to increase self-awareness and individual ownership of the approaches to resolve the issues (Jones, n.d.).

Conversely, mentoring encompasses a more informal and spontaneous relationship focused on reciprocating symbiotic relationships offering long-term career improvement benefiting both mentor and recipient (ATD, n.d.). Mentoring educators empowers both the mentor and the recipient to pose questions, share possibilities, and advance both the outcomes and the relationship (Jones, n.d.).

Ultimately, establishing a single relationship that integrates coaching and mentoring generates optimal opportunities for everyone. Therefore, in this chapter focused on guiding and supporting teacher candidates, the words *mentor* and *coach* will be used together, allowing the reader to apply the most appropriate scenario to each relationship, as shown in figure 3.1. Collectively, mentoring and coaching contribute to establishing a firm foundation promoting character development holistically in the teacher candidate accompanied by the dedication of time and energy (Emory University, n.d.), benefiting both the candidate and the coach.

Although the mentoring process may seem natural and authentic, similar challenges exist for both candidates and coaches yet experienced through opposing viewpoints. Candidates are challenged by their lack of knowledge, skills, and dispositions in becoming teachers; their awareness, actions, and attitudes tend to be developmentally appropriate, aligned with their completion of preparation courses and field experiences. Most candidates are focused on immediate concerns related to course assignments. Additionally, candidates range in their comfort levels as they embark on their new careers.

LEAP INTO MENTORING TEACHER CANDIDATES

The definition of *leap* is to jump or spring a long way—a word that captures the attitudes and actions a teacher educator should possess when mentoring/coaching teacher candidates. The approach to mentoring offered here is called LEAP, an acronym whose letters represent the words Listen and Learn, Engage and Excite, Adapt and Adopt, and Practice and Promote. Building upon the definition, LEAP equips and empowers the teacher educator serving as a mentor to soar and overcome the candidate's encountered situations and perceived obstacles. Each component of LEAP is essential, and the four components should be considered holistically for this approach to mentoring/coaching to be most effective.

Listen and Learn. The act of listening requires full attention and concentration without interruption. Many mentors find the act of listening difficult as they are focused on the words or messages they want to say or the questions they want to ask rather than absorbing and remembering the speaker's message. Through active listening, frequently the mentor learns about the teacher candidate's real and imagined concerns from the perspective of the candidate. This discovery is imperative for the mentor to completely understand the candidate.

The mentor should avoid viewing the candidate's perspectives exclusively as a teacher educator supplemented with lists of tasks and instant solutions. Listening and learning encompasses a well-honed, all-embracing one-

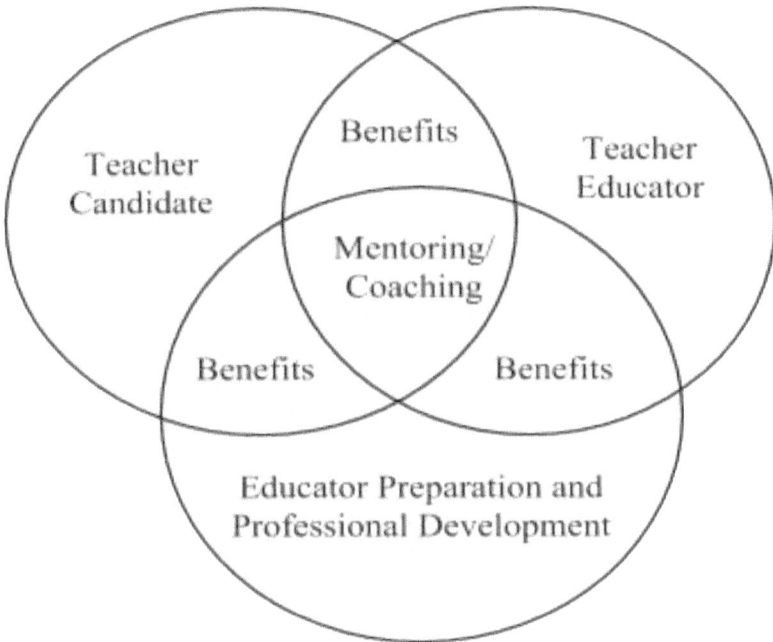

Figure 3.1. Benefits of Mentoring and Coaching for Teacher Candidates, Teacher Educators, and Educator Preparation and Professional Development

ness with the candidate in order for the candidate to both trust the mentor and to return for future mentorship with the teacher educator.

Engage and Excite. While listening to the candidate, the mentor must ascertain the relevant moments and select the appropriate words to engage the candidate. The mentor is encouraged to initiate conversation with either a general opener or a specific reference to a previous conversation or event. When the candidate senses trust and sincerity from the mentor, most likely the candidate will share concerns and pose questions.

As with active listening, the mentor must express authentic engagement. Being aware of the relevant moments to delve encourages the candidate to share additional information that frequently helps both the mentor and the candidate to isolate the cause of a concern and identify ways to manage and/ or cope with the concern.

Additionally, selecting the appropriate words when delving is imperative to both encourage and excite the candidate to build resilience and motivate action. Although the mentor may be willing and able to resolve some situations for the candidate, the mentor must be cognizant of deflecting tasks back to the candidate for the candidate to resolve independently. The most effective way for the candidate to grow and develop is to be provided the techniques, tools, and tips for understanding and overcoming challenges and changes.

Adapt and Adopt. This component of LEAP offers useful guidance and constructive support for both the candidate and the mentor. As the relationship between candidate and mentor advances, their shared understanding and interactions transform. Ideally, the candidate adapts some of the perspectives (specifically the targets, techniques, tools, and tips) offered by the mentor, and the mentor adapts some of the perspectives (anticipated concerns and challenges) experienced by the candidate.

Becoming familiar with their interactions, both the candidate and the mentor begin to adopt or accept the flow of their relationship. The outcomes from adapting to new situations, that is, challenges, allow the candidate and the mentor to reinforce their initial sense of openness to one of evolving ideas and expectations; adopting new strategies associated with change inspires individuals to expand their intellectual horizons, consider new possibilities, and increase their sense of competence and confidence.

Practice and Promote. The final component of LEAP both reinforces the previous three components (Listen and Learn, Engage and Excite, Adapt and Adopt) with pragmatic applications and advances the entire approach of LEAP in ways that are natural and holistic. The roles and responsibilities of the mentor anticipate that the mentor recognizes and appreciates the background of the candidate, that is, UTCB, UTCM, or GTCM, and demands associated with the candidate's particular academic goals and educator preparation program. Candidates in all three groups (UTCB, UTCM, and GTCM) are experiencing unique ages and stages of life in relationship to the dynamics of professionals: their personal growth, professional development, pedagogical expertise, and political astuteness, as shown in table 3.1.

The mentor should be prepared to provide practices by co-constructing knowledge, skills, and dispositions with the candidate that contribute to the candidate's self-efficacy and sense of agency, two desired qualities of career educators. The practice and promotion of self-efficacy (Bandura, 1977) empower the candidate to develop a sense of responsibility and competence to contribute to the growth and development of all learners and is grounded in

- content and pedagogical knowledge,
- guided clinical experiences with diverse students in diverse settings,
- collaborative learning communities,
- authentic assessment and reflective decision making, and
- professional integrity including leadership, collaboration, and service. (UCA College of Education, 2015)

Simultaneously by developing a sense of agency (Bandura, 1989) or ownership, candidates begin to understand the power they possess as individuals,

Table 3.1. Today's Teacher Candidates in Relationship to Dynamics of Professionals: Personal Growth, Professional Development, Pedagogical Expertise, and Political Astuteness

	UTCB	UTCM	GTCM
Personal Growth	Teenager to young adult Living at home or at school May be working part-time	Young adult to older adult Living on own Working full-time	Young adult to older adult Family of own Working in a career
Professional Development	Basic experience Little to no time in schools	Multifaceted experience May have worked in a P–12 school	Advanced experience Earned a college degree May have children in a P–12 school
Pedagogical Expertise	Limited understanding Coursework new	Limited understanding Coursework new	Limited understanding Coursework new
Political Astuteness	Initial awareness First-time voter	Initial awareness First- or second-time voter	Varied awareness Voter May have attended or served in a political position

as parts of current systems (that is, educator preparation program), and as parts of future systems (that is, career professionals in relationship to the dynamics of professionalism). Mentors can be instrumental in helping candidates practice and promote their self-efficacy and agency as they leap from candidate to career.

The four components of LEAP (Listen and Learn, Engage and Excite, Adapt and Adopt, Practice and Promote) are accompanied by ten essential elements that guide and support teacher educators as mentors, as shown in table 3.2. These ten elements have been generated through my own extensive mentoring with teacher candidates, doctoral candidates, and university colleagues. Teacher educators serving as mentors and coaches will discover various elements are more critical as they mentor and are encouraged to try all ten essential elements.

BENEFITS OF MENTORING AND COACHING

Mentoring and coaching offer benefits for teacher candidates, teacher educators, and educator preparation and professional development, as shown in

Table 3.2. LEAP Elements

Element	Guidance	Support
Time	Ask when convenient for mentor and candidate. Schedule a dedicated time. Schedule the next meeting at the end of the current meeting.	*Respect*
Focus	Meet in a mutually agreed-upon space. Move away from other people, desks, computers, phones, and other electronics. Do not close the door completely. Place a sign on the door that you are mentoring.	*Importance*
Welcome	Offer water and check lighting and temperature. Sit in comfortable chairs.	*Comfort*
Readiness	Keep notepad, pen, clock, and schedule handy. Take notes occasionally.	*Reassurance*
Dialogue	Ask questions, offer advice, and add examples. Allow/encourage candidate to ask questions. Contextualize guidance and talk freely. Remember to listen and not dominate the conversation.	*Sincerity*
Development	Clarify understanding and co-construct possibilities. Cultivate reflectivity for the candidate to • describe occurring concerns; • explain ways the concerns are affecting the candidate personally, professionally, pedagogically, and politically; • probe reasons the concerns are affecting the candidate; • explore ways for the candidate to manage the concerns interdependently at first, then moving to independently with time, practice, and promotion; • offer reasons the concerns should be managed by the candidate; • imagine possibilities for coping with concerns, that is, managing the current concerns or when encountering future concerns.	*Trust*
Feedback	Provide meaningful feedback to the candidate. Feedback must • make personalized connections (use the candidate's name), • be contextualized appropriately, • reinforce achievements, • offer motivation.	*Confidence*

Element	Guidance	Support
Goals	Help the candidate to set achievable goals. Goals must be short term and evidence based. You must monitor and ask about the set goals.	*Competence*
Communication	Initiate communication with the candidate, especially when the candidate does not initiate or maintain communication with the teacher educator.	*Encouragement*
Advancement	As the candidate demonstrates understanding and achievement of one goal, set another goal and repeat the process to advance the dynamics of professionalism.	*Accomplishment*

figure 3.1. Teacher candidates gain confidence and competence associated with their personal growth, professional development, pedagogical expertise, and political astuteness that contribute to their aspirations as they transition from becoming a teacher to being a teacher. In reciprocity, teacher educators gain insights and inspirations that not only increase their abilities to listen and learn, engage and excite, adapt and adopt, and practice and promote self-efficacy and agency in their candidates, but also realize they have advanced their own dynamics of professionalism.

Capitalizing on the ten essential elements of mentoring, teacher educators hear concerns and comments from candidates that help teacher educators improve educator preparation and professional development. Improvements to programs and policies can increase student enrollment and retention as well as enhance career development and resiliency.

Ultimately, as teacher educators become more aware of today's teacher candidates coupled with their own roles and responsibilities as mentor/coaches advocated in the LEAP approach, teacher educators advance their own self-efficacy and sense of agency in ways that build their confidence, competence, and commitment to their own career professionalism.

SUMMARY

Increasingly, teacher educators are becoming more aware of and committed to their endeavors associated with coaching and mentoring teacher candidates. The goals are to increase their candidates' engagement and achievement (self-efficacy) coupled with enhancing candidates' professionalism and retention (agency). To develop their roles and responsibilities, teacher educators are encouraged to explore the LEAP approach.

The four components of LEAP (Listen and Learn, Engage and Excite, Adapt and Adopt, Practice and Promote) are characterized by ten elements accompanied by a specific guide and support for mentors as they coach their undergraduate and graduate teacher candidates and gain insights and inspiration to advance their own professionalism.

QUESTIONS FOR REFLECTION

1. What are the roles and responsibilities associated with mentoring and coaching?
2. What are the conditions and concerns of

   - the undergraduate teacher candidate basic?
   - the undergraduate teacher candidate multifaceted?
   - the graduate teacher candidate multifaceted?

3. How does mentoring impact and benefit

   - teacher candidates?
   - teacher educators?

Chapter Four

A Triad of Instructional Coaching

Changing Classroom Practices

Michelle Buchanan, MAT, NBCT,
University of Central Arkansas

Today's dynamic classrooms require teachers to provide learning opportunities that promote active student participation and support meaningful discussions by serving as facilitators in learning and working collaboratively with students (National Board of Professional Teaching Standards, 2016). It is important for teacher preparation programs to assist teacher candidates in preparing for this changing role. Through a triad of instructional coaching support, teacher candidates can be better prepared to facilitate active and engaged learning in today's classrooms.

Throughout their teacher education program, teacher candidates become peer coaches to each other during their early field experiences, they receive coaching from their university instructors, and they are coached by their cooperating classroom teachers during their practicum and internship experiences.

It is through these instructional coaching experiences that a teacher candidate grows personally, professionally, and pedagogically, through the "processes of accepting, acquiring, and applying requisite knowledge, skills, and dispositions for ensuring educational equity and excellence for all learners" (Gallavan, 2007, p. 6).

This chapter will discuss the ways in which teacher preparation programs can provide early and embedded guidance and support for teacher candidates, resulting in classroom teachers who are more reflective and effective educators seeking continual improvement in their craft. Their experiences with instructional coaching will also increase the likelihood they will be prepared to assume the role of coaching to facilitate student learning in their future classrooms.

While this chapter includes scenarios about mathematics and science teacher candidates, the instructional coaching illustrated in the examples are applicable to all teacher candidates, encouraging reflective teaching, providing practice in peer coaching, and receiving and applying coaching from a more experienced educator.

COACHING TEACHER CANDIDATES

Creating instructional coaches requires modeling at the teacher candidate education level, thus applying the *isomorphism principle*: teachers should be educated in the same way that they are expected to teach (Ponte and Chapman, 2008). In early field experiences, teacher candidates have several opportunities to observe their cooperating teacher.

As teacher candidates progress through the education program, teacher candidates assume increasingly higher levels of responsibility in their field experiences, from tutoring individual pupils to teaching small groups during instructional time. Eventually they plan and teach whole-class lessons, and this is where the first level of the coaching triad, peer coaching, is introduced.

In a reciprocal peer coaching model, teacher candidates observe each other and offer feedback to improve their peer's instruction. They provide each other with suggestions, assistance, and support. Peer coaches should work as co-teachers, not evaluators; candidates independently create and implement lessons, but they should collaborate with each other in the different stages of lesson planning, implementation, and evaluation.

Peer coaching benefits teacher candidates two significant ways: (1) learning from observing, providing feedback, and reflecting on their partner's instruction, and (2) learning from their peer's observation and feedback to improve their instruction. Additional benefits of peer coaching in a teacher education program include (a) positive feedback among peers, (b) suggestions to improve instruction, (c) commonality and sharing of experiences, (d) development of self-confidence, and (e) less intimidation during the observation process (Kurtts and Levin, 2000).

Bowman and McCormick (2000) found teacher candidates in a reciprocal peer coaching program increased the clarity of their instruction and increased their pedagogical reasoning and action skills. Teacher candidates who utilize peer and instructional coaching and reflective practices can be better prepared for their role as facilitator or coach in the classroom.

The cooperating teacher and university supervising teacher serve as experts in the second and third levels of the instructional coaching triad. Expert coaching models involve a coach that is viewed as a more experienced other in the particular area of need, such as content, pedagogy, or classroom management.

Typically, instructional coaches observe, model, provide feedback, and plan lessons; the tasks depend on the needs and goals of the individual teacher candidate. Depending on the type of professional development needed, the instructional coach may be the listener, the more experienced other, or the learner on the side.

The use of the expert coaching model is especially important in content areas that require laboratory and authentic learning investigations. For example, mathematics and science teacher candidates need experience collaborating with veteran classroom teachers regarding use and management of equipment with the students, classroom management procedures in a lab-based setting, and performance-based assessments—to name a few. Ideally, this coaching relationship should occur before the culminating internship course.

Early field experiences involving coaching by veteran teachers will alleviate some of the concerns teacher candidates have when they first enter a classroom. The more opportunities teacher candidates have to apply their knowledge and skills in the classroom, the better prepared they will be for internship and their teaching career. Furthermore, coaching teacher candidates has multiple benefits including reducing discouragement, isolation, and frustration often typical of new teachers (McAllister and Neubert, 1995).

COACHING USING REFLECTIVE TEACHING

Effective teachers cannot be created singularly by the act of teaching; powerful teachers are created by the act of reflecting (Danielson et al., 2009). Instructional coaching in teacher preparation programs can be enhanced with video reflective practices through (1) video case reflections, (2) self-reflections on a teacher's own video-recorded practices, and (3) reflecting with a peer group on teachers' own video-recorded practices.

Educating teacher candidates using video reflection and annotation can help increase the knowledge and the competencies involved in becoming a teacher. These observations through video can include the teacher candidate's professionalism (organized and prepared to teach, punctuality, professional dress, etc.), lesson delivery (objectives achieved, students' understanding, student engagement, content is accurate, etc.), interactions (encourages student discourse, gives feedback to all students, etc.), and logistics (maintains order, maximizes learning time).

Conversations with an instructional coach using video reflection can provide teacher candidates valuable growth opportunities by helping them to analyze events, link theory to practice, expand pedagogical repertoires, and make complex decisions (Arya, Christ, and Chiu, 2013). Another incentive for using video to improve teaching practices with instructional coaching is time constraints. Sometimes scheduling a time when two classroom teachers can meet to converse for instructional coaching can be difficult.

Video-recorded lessons offer the opportunities for teachers to discuss the observation together without being in the same room. Teachers can view the recorded video and add comments at their most convenient time of the day and still provide effective coaching.

Charlotte Danielson's renowned framework for teaching analysis, assessing teaching practice, and ultimately assisting in teacher improvement is used internationally in teacher preparation, instructional coaching, and professional development (Danielson et al., 2009). Danielson's framework for teaching (2009) breaks teaching practice into four domains with twenty-two components and seventy-six subcomponents.

- Domain 1: Planning and Preparation
- Domain 2: Classroom Environment
- Domain 3: Instruction
- Domain 4: Professional Responsibilities

Domain 4 focuses on reflective teaching and professional development. Reflective teaching encompasses thinking about what happened in the classroom during a teaching experience, and reflective teaching is made easier with video annotation.

Here are some examples of video reflection questions teacher candidates can answer based on field experiences:

- Where are your lesson objective(s) represented in the video? Remember to use a measurable verb that describes the learning. ("Students will . . .") What domain(s) and component(s) are represented in this answer, and how do they relate to this answer?
- What was the highlight of your lesson (that impacted student learning)? What evidence do you have to support your answers?
- What would you do differently if you taught the lesson again, and why? What domain(s) and component(s) are represented in this answer, and how do they relate to this answer?
- Think about your questioning. Did you ask questions on a variety of thinking levels? Were your questions mostly open ended? What domain(s) and component(s) are represented in this answer, and how do they relate to this answer?
- How have you grown since your previous teaching experience? What pedagogical knowledge did you use to improve your teaching? What domain(s) and component(s) are represented in this answer, and how do they relate to this answer?

- Articulate and justify your goals for your next lesson. What areas would you like to improve on for your next teaching experience: giving clear directions, wait time, using developed questions, attention-getting strategies, pacing of lesson, and/or materials management? What domain(s) and component(s) are represented in this answer, and how do they relate to this answer?

In summary, it is important that the instructional coach helps the teacher candidate measure performance periodically through observations as he or she develops new skills through the application of pedagogy. In other words, "coaching without the study of theory, the observation of demonstrations, and opportunities for practice with feedback will, in fact, accomplish very little" (Joyce and Showers, 1981, p. 5).

PRACTICAL APPLICATION IN THE FIELD

Changing how teachers teach happens when teacher candidates' needs are met at the instructional level. Additionally, teacher candidates need a triad of instructional coaching relationships to better prepare them as they enter the classroom.

Imagine two high school teacher candidates enrolled in a university: Justine is a mathematics major and Shaquille is a chemistry major. They both take courses in the college of education through a minor program designed specifically for mathematics and science majors. The program establishes strong connections between mathematics and science and between educational theory and practice.

In one of their university education classes, their instructor assigns peer coaches—fellow classmates who coach one another, provide companionship, and contribute feedback and ideas as they strive to meet the individual needs of the students they will teach. In other words, the university class has a coaching environment in which every teacher candidate sees themselves as each other's coaches. Justine is paired with another mathematics major and Shaquille is paired with another science major so that they may more easily collaborate with similar field experiences.

The coaching models in the following scenarios offer the teacher candidates experiences that formatively assess their teaching and also encourage reflective practice and responsive teaching that should carry over to their own classrooms.

COACHING SCENARIO WITH JUSTINE

Justine is a mathematics major placed in a tenth-grade geometry class for early field placement. She has been give the mathematics content standard by her cooperating classroom teacher: "CCSS.MATH.CONTENT.HSG.SRT.A.3 Use the properties of similarity transformations to establish the AA criterion for two triangles to be congruent—if two angles of one triangle are the same as two angles of another triangle, then the triangles are the same size" (National Governors Association Center for Best Practices, 2010, para. 3).

Justine looks forward to sharing her passion for mathematics with her students. The first task assigned by Justine's university instructor is to design a pre-assessment that will allow her to understand (1) what the students know about the concept (including foundational knowledge) and (2) what interests the students have outside of the mathematics classroom.

After Justine has prepared a short list of questions she spends time in class with her university peer coach to evaluate the effectiveness of her pre-assessment activity. Justine and her college peers are practicing a process that encourages professional collaboration and personal reflection. This coaching strategy provides Justine and her peers an opportunity for support and feedback, and it teaches the value of teacher leadership early in their teacher preparation.

When Justine, her peer coach, and her university instructor are satisfied with the pre-assessment, she submits it to her cooperating teacher for another opportunity to collaborate with a more experienced other. After these collaborations, Justine implements and evaluates the pre-assessment results. Then she begins the second task: developing the lesson plan based on the 5E lesson design.

Back in her university class, Justine and her peer coach each take time to discuss the results of their pre-assessments and how the data helped them to formulate their lesson plans. Justine's peer coach listens to her describe the nonacademic results from her pre-assessment. For example, many of the students are involved in competitive sports. Her peer coach provides detailed instructional feedback with specific praise and asks clarifying questions about Justine's data and lesson ideas.

Justine's peer coach has the idea for her to play a game for the "Elaborate" part of the lesson. By allowing the teacher candidates to plan together, a dynamic discussion can occur about teaching practices through the role of coaching. The teaching experience includes planning, implementation, assessment, and extension.

When teacher candidates consider how each of these components affects learners mastering content knowledge, they can then differentiate between the strategies and activities that will effectively further learning and those that need revisions. Justine decides to model a game for her students after

Illuminations Triangle Classification lesson (Zordak, 2016). She feels she can have better success in motivating the students to be engaged in the lesson as they discover relationships through their experiences in the game. This lesson is next digitally shared with her cooperating classroom teacher and university instructor so that the three of them can have a discussion about the components of the lesson.

The cooperating classroom teacher collaborates with Justine during the game creation, assisting her with the game design and play execution. Because this will be the first time Justine will facilitate a lesson with game play, her university supervisor coaches her in management strategies to use while the students play the game to maximize the learning opportunity. This three-way collaboration helps Justine with constructive and encouraging feedback concerning her lesson development, and this encouragement helps her confidence to deliver a student-discovery lesson.

After Justine teaches her lesson, she reviews her recorded video and begins to reflect on the teaching experience. She identifies the lesson's objectives and annotates where they can be observed in the video using the video annotation software. She states that domain 1 (Danielson et al., 2009) is represented with designing coherent instruction because her learning activities allowed for student success in mastering the standard. Justine really enjoyed seeing the students have fun with the game. Their laughter throughout that portion of the lesson was the evidence she used to show that she created an environment of respect and rapport.

Justine reflected on the types of questions she asked and saw that she asked more single-answer questions. To her dismay she noticed that she also answered her own questions before giving the students a chance to share their responses. Justine knows that she needs to improve the quality of her questions and discussion techniques.

Justine had various coaches to help her during this early field experience. She and her peer coach searched for ways to reach common goals as they collaborated. Through their feedback sessions, her university classroom cooperating teacher served as the more experienced other. Her university supervisor and classroom cooperating teacher served as coaches when they helped Justine become more thoughtful and more effective in her instruction.

The instructional coaching triad Justine experienced was highly effective because it was relevant to what she was preparing to teach, allowed her to immediately implement what she was learning, provided feedback focused on improving her lesson in terms of teaching strategies, and evaluated student engagement and the effectiveness of assessment.

COACHING SCENARIO WITH SHAQUILLE

Shaquille is a chemistry major placed in a ninth-grade physical science class for early field placement. Shaquille has confidence in his knowledge of chemistry, but he has never had the opportunity to set up, conduct, and evaluate a lab exercise for students. "Playing this critical role requires that teacher know much more than how to set up equipment, carry out procedures, and manage students' physical activities. Teachers must consider how to integrate laboratory experiences into the stream of instruction and how to select individual laboratory activities that will fit most appropriately into their science classes" (National Research Council [NRC], 2006, p. 140).

As a chemistry major, Shaquille has set up, performed, and analyzed the data from countless tests in his college career thus far. He understands the importance of safety, and he knows that lab experiences are an important step in developing an understanding of scientific concepts. The first task assigned by Shaquille's university instructor is to communicate with his cooperating teacher about the needs of the students he will teach. His cooperating teacher states that the class struggles with the content and has several English language–learning students.

Shaquille has been given the science content standard by his cooperating classroom teacher: "HS-PS1-4 Develop a model to illustrate that the release or absorption of energy from a chemical reaction system depends upon the changes in total bond energy" (NGSS Lead States, 2013, para. 4). Shaquille would like the students to conduct a lab exercise, but Shaquille's cooperating classroom teacher encourages Shaquille to think beyond the students conducting a lab to meet this standard.

While his cooperating teacher agrees that science curriculum cannot teach itself, his cooperating teacher shares with him that modeling can take multiple forms: demonstrations, physical models, drawings, etc. His cooperating teacher points out that the model should be on a molecular level. Soon Shaquille begins to see how a lab report might not allow all of the students to communicate their understanding as deeply or as well as some other form of expression.

As Shaquille plans his lesson and receives assistance from his peer coach, together they develop the idea for the students to use stop-motion video to model their understanding of what happens at the molecular level during simple chemical reactions. Shaquille meets with his university instructor to organize the development of the lesson. Together they decide to create a multiday lesson based on a lesson he found on BetterClassroom.com (Hill, 2017).

Shaquille creates a stop-motion video to determine how much time the students will need. His university instructor coaches him to provide the students the opportunity to choose a chemical reaction of their choice to en-

courage student engagement and relevancy. The first day will focus on reviewing the components of chemical reactions and where they can be found in the students' lives.

He plans to share with the students their video assignment to demonstrate their knowledge. He prepares several online resources for the students to use if they have difficulty choosing a chemical reaction. The students will spend three days creating storyboards, scripts, and sets for the videos. On day four, students will evaluate their product using these criteria:

- The model (stop-motion video) correctly shows a chemical reaction occurring.
- The molecular structure correctly identifies chemical reactions, reactants, and products.
- The model correctly explains conservation of matter and molecular rearrangement.

Day five is the last day, and the students will show their videos to the class, where their peers evaluate the content for accuracy. In this lesson, Shaquille will act in the role of a facilitator providing a learning opportunity for the students to build an understanding of the content that only comes from inquiry learning.

After the lesson is presented, Shaquille and his cooperating classroom teacher sit down to reflect on and discuss student engagement and understanding of the content. The cooperating classroom teacher asks him how the project supported English language learners without limiting the students who need additional challenges in a way that a lab report could not. As his coach, his cooperating classroom teacher encourages Shaquille to reflect on how all students correctly demonstrated their understanding of how energy is released from a chemical reaction system. Their conversation progresses and Shaquille begins to think about specific aspects of the lesson that impacted all students' learning.

After Shaquille teaches his lesson, he reviews his recorded video and begins to reflect on the teaching experience. He really enjoyed seeing the students dive deeper into the content more than just what a lab exercise would allow; he observed the English language learners did not need to spend time translating their video as their animation completely demonstrated their understanding of the content.

Student pride in their work throughout the development of the video and during presentation day was the evidence he used to show that he established a culture for learning. He reflected on the types of questions he asked and saw that the stop-motion videos allowed him to ask thought-provoking questions, and this has him striving to continue asking quality questions to host discussions deep in content.

Shaquille also benefited from three levels of instructional coaching. Serving as the more experienced other, his classroom cooperating teacher served as his coach when he helped Shaquille become a more creative thinker about how to access students' deeper understanding of the content. Shaquille's coaching experience was relevant to what he was preparing to teach, allowed him to immediately implement what he was learning, offered feedback focused on improving his lesson in terms of teaching strategies, and evaluated student engagement and the effectiveness of assessment.

While he was initially disappointed in not being able to conduct a lab investigation, his cooperating classroom teacher coached him on choosing lesson activities that best enabled the students to meet the standard. As in the case of Justine, the triad of instructional coaching and reflection encouraged Shaquille to continue to strive for instructional improvement early in his teacher education career.

CLASSROOM TEACHERS COACH THEIR STUDENTS

Instilling reflective teaching and coaching as professional development during early field experiences—such as in Justine's and Shaquille's scenarios—encourages long-term buy-in for continuous and reflective improvement and a changing role of the teacher: classroom teachers serving as coaches to their students. Recent changes in the national mathematics and science content standards have required teachers to shift from traditional classroom instruction to that which is more focused on problem solving and inquiry instead of rote memorization.

Mathematics and science teachers are becoming learners beside their students in authentic learning environments as students are no longer docile recipients of information. Instead of students passively receiving information through rote lessons from their teachers, students collaborate with each other to develop a solution and understanding of the content, discuss their understandings with each other and the teacher, and reflect on their learning, all with teacher support.

While the classroom teacher has extensive knowledge of a specific content area (specifically discussing mathematics and science fields), the Internet provides today's students a plethora of information that meets students' specific interests as it relates to the content being learned. It is this simple fact that challenges teachers to separate from the traditional classroom model, where the teacher imparts the necessary information to the students.

In an effort to keep students engaged, teachers enter the coaching role. They personalize learning and model the teacher and student partnership in education; these allow students to be more self-directed and self-disciplined.

As science and mathematics teachers change their mindset to that of a coaching role, teachers and their students search for ways to reach common goals.

SUMMARY

More than thirty years of research on teacher professional development identifies the power of teacher collaboration in improving teaching instruction and student learning (NRC, 2006). Instructional coaching can be the catalyst that causes teacher candidates to eventually evolve into the more experienced teacher role and into another instructional coach. To increase the effectiveness of this professional development, many recommend teacher candidates receive embedded and long-term support through models such as instructional coaching (Aguilar, 2013; Appleton, 2008).

For coaching to be effective at making lasting changes in the classroom (and also in the classroom of all teachers), Butler et al. (2004) recommended coaching be relevant to what the students are learning, allow the teacher to immediately implement what was learned, occur over a sustained time to increase teacher buy-in, and use feedback to focus on improving the lesson in terms of teaching strategies, student engagement, and assessment to guide instruction.

To further increase effectiveness and meet criteria recommended by Butler et al. (2004), an ongoing professional, and even personal, relationship should be established between the coach and teacher. The relationship should be conceived of mutual trust, respect, and collegiality. Instructional coaching relationships offer support for teacher candidates, for teachers in the early stages of their careers, and for teachers needing guidance and support with specific classroom challenges.

Coaching participants plan and discuss appropriate strategies to address the needs of all learners, allow for immediate implementation, and engage in continuous conversations that focus on improvement, student engagement, and assessment effectiveness. As seen in Justine's and Shaquille's scenarios, the collaborative conversations with the instructional coaching triad (peer coaches, university instructors, and cooperating classroom teachers) suggest the effectiveness of the instructional coaching at the three different levels. Their instructional coaches at each level assisted them in preparing, teaching, and analytically reflecting on their lessons.

The conversations with their coaches helped them develop teaching skills by preparing and implementing inquiry lessons to meet identified standards. Their coaches also encouraged the teacher candidates to stretch their thoughts about the role of a teacher to include that of learning facilitator. Their lessons allowed for personalized learning, and they created learning opportunities that allowed students to be more student directed and student disciplined in learning the content. Like these two scenarios, coaching can represent one-on-one encounters within the coaching triad, but coaches can also work with groups or teams of teachers.

QUESTIONS FOR REFLECTION

1. Teachers "think systematically about their practice and learn from experience" using video (National Board of Professional Teaching Standards, 2016). Coaches should always plan with teacher candidates before working in their classrooms. Coaches should begin the collaboration so that the teacher candidate gets a better sense of how to approach the lesson. How could Justine's university instructor and peer coach help her to improve her reflective practice?
2. Not only do teachers (as do teachers of all subject areas) help students develop scientific reasoning (logical thinking), understand the content, and guide and focus discussions and reflections within individuals, laboratory groups (small groups), and the entire class, but they also address logistical and practical concerns such as obtaining and safely storing supplies and maintaining laboratory safety (NRC, 2006). Unfortunately, "pre-service education and in-service professional development for science teachers rarely address laboratory experiences and do not provide teachers with the knowledge and skills needed to lead laboratory experiences" (NRC, 2006, p. 138). How could Shaquille's university instructor and cooperating classroom teacher help him to improve his ability develop and conduct labs for high schools students?

Chapter Five

Virtual Coaching of Teacher Candidates

Using BIE to Supervise and Support Interns in a Teacher Preparation Program

Tammy R. Benson, EdD,
University of Central Arkansas

The coffee is hot, the couch is comfy, and my computer is in my lap. As I wait for the Skype call to ring in, I am thankful that our early morning test run went well. In comes the call from Sheri, who is teaching a third-grade classroom in a small rural community some 106 miles away. She has Skype set up on an iPad and she is using a Swivl that allows the iPad to rotate and follow her as she moves around her classroom. At first, I'm seeing a lot of ceiling, but with a slight adjustment made by Sheri, I now see the entire classroom clearly.

On my computer screen, I have Sheri's lesson plan displayed on half of my computer screen and can see her teaching in real time on the other half. There are a couple of the students that smile and wave at me when they notice me on the iPad screen. I smile and wave back and, to minimize student distractions, I quickly click the camera icon to blank out the screen.

We test the sound from the bug in the ear (BIE) and establish that it is working great—she can hear me and I can hear her and the students. I have to remember that she can hear everything I say, even a sigh, so I mute the speaker when I am not giving feedback. I start out trying to encourage her in what she is doing. It feels a little intrusive to be the bug in her ear. Some of the feedback and prompts that I use to encourage and redirect Sheri's instruction include:

Buzz about—that's a creative way to assign them to discuss—was that your idea? Have they ever made a story map before? Could you give them the example of a best supporting actor in a movie like the Academy Awards? Be consistent on calling on those that raise hands if that is your procedure. Does each partner have their own paper or are they sharing? Have they preread these chapters? Can you slow down a little for the group in the back? Remember the higher-level questions—compare, why, how, etc. Slow down when you are reading.

The children were very excited about a book they were reading and all seemed engaged with the lesson activities. At the end of the lesson, a young girl went to the teacher and hugged her, telling her that she "smelled like rainbows and happiness." She asked, "Do you shower in rainbows and happiness?" It was at that moment with a bit of sadness that I realized the one thing I was missing with this comfy little virtual coaching experience was the children.

As a supervisor with a background in elementary education, I was accustomed to interacting with the children while I supervised my interns. As convenient as this virtual observation was, I missed being there for the "rainbows and happiness"! This was my first experience with virtual coaching. I was very excited that I could actually provide coaching to my student from my own living room—wow, how technology has changed our world.

Throughout the evolution of education, various methods of teacher training have emerged to provide innovative approaches to improve teaching and learning. Teacher education faculty are always searching for ways to increase the quality of feedback and assessment of teacher education candidates. One method is the model of peer coaching, recommended to improve teacher effectiveness in recent years (Cotabish et al., 2013; Joyce and Showers, 1996). The traditional goal of peer coaching is to provide positive feedback to instructors; however, more recently the peer coach has a greater responsibility, including more guidance, modeling, and facilitating classroom lessons.

Teachers have indicated that observing and talking to their coaches and receiving classroom support from their coaches has been instrumental in changing their teaching instruction (Gustafson, Guilbert, and MacDonald, 2002). Moreover, peer coaching teams have been found to promote school-wide change and more skillful staff development by facilitating a strong cohesiveness among teachers and allowing for more shared decision making (Joyce and Showers, 1996).

In recent years, an innovative technology-driven approach to coaching has offered an interesting opportunity. With the increased demand for universities to provide online programming options for students, innovative and cost-effective approaches for instructional delivery are a high priority. To respond to the demand, virtual peer coaching innovations are becoming increasingly popular with pre-service teacher candidates during practicum and semester-long internships.

This chapter will describe one teacher preparation program's experience with implementing virtual coaching in their culminating internship course detailing logistics, benefits and limitations, and suggestions for future implications for field supervision of classroom teachers (Benson and Cotabish, 2014; Wake et al., in press).

VIRTUAL COACHING DEFINED

The landscape of teacher education has changed significantly in recent years and the pressure to provide accountability for teacher education programs has never been higher. Educators search for ways to help teacher candidates be successful in the most efficient, cost-effective way possible. Virtual coaching is a way to receive the benefits of peer coaching but from a distance without having your *feet on the ground*. This approach uses online and mobile technology to allow a coach located in the building or across the country to observe and offer discreet, running feedback to the teacher who wears an earpiece during the lesson.

Virtual coaching involves using innovative technology such as BIE wireless Bluetooth headsets and adapters, camera or iPad, and recording software to conduct peer coaching. Using this technology, supervisors can watch a lesson going on in the classroom at any time and for as many times as needed. Teacher candidates are given multiple opportunities to receive immediate feedback from their supervisor as the supervisor provides constructive feedback throughout the lesson in real time, much like watching a news reporter receive breaking news from his or her headset and then reporting the breaking news directly to the listeners.

Teacher candidates receive prompts, encouragement, cautions, and reminders in the moment they are teaching their students. In this way, they can receive the feedback from their supervisor, monitor and adjust what they are doing, and improve the instructional delivery of lessons. This technology removes the barrier of distance and allows more teachers to receive the benefits and increased frequency of coaching interactions.

SETTING UP A VIRTUAL COACHING EXPERIENCE

Recently, a Master of Arts in Teaching (MAT) program implemented a virtual coaching experience during the culminating internship course. The MAT program is a nontraditional program in which those with degrees in other areas without a teaching license progress through a graduate program of pedagogy to fulfill requirements for a license to teach in Arkansas. Many of these students live in rural areas of the state, many miles from the campus in Conway, Arkansas. It seemed promising to offer virtual coaching to these students to explore the implications on their teaching effectiveness and to better manage faculty time and resources.

The MAT intervention started with only eight candidates who volunteered to use the BIE technology for their internship supervision with two supervisors and has progressed to the current practice that all MAT internship candidates with teaching positions on provisional licenses use the BIE technology. Currently, twelve university supervisors have utilized the BIE technology to supervise their interns. The only candidates not utilizing the BIE technology are the ones without teaching jobs who are placed in schools. These candidates and their assigned K–12 school mentors prefer more direct, face-to-face contact through regular visits with the university supervisor.

Prior to the implementation of the intervention, candidates complete a two-hour professional development workshop focused on the observation rubric used to evaluate teacher candidates' instruction (Danielson, 2007) and receive directions and demonstrations on using the BIE technology under simulated conditions. Supervisors test the technology and then provide a specific, detailed list of directions to guide candidates through setting up and using the technology.

Candidates also participate in case scenarios, giving them practice adapting to the technology, problem solving, and working through various technological challenges. Each student is provided a Cirago Bluetooth 3.0 USB Micro Adapter, Web Cam, Plantronics M50 Bluetooth Headset (BIE device), and instructed to create a Skype account. Supervisors and interns share Skype accounts and schedule practice sessions before the first observation to make sure that all technology is working properly because some schools have barriers set up to block Internet connections.

Knowing that virtual mentoring relationships are challenging and can be a little slower to develop, as reported by Owen (2015), efforts are made to form trust and open communication on the front end to ensure a strong mentor/mentee relationship throughout the semester. After the workshop, the candidates participate in a semester-long teaching internship requiring three formal observations (two BIE observations and one videotaped observation) conducted by a university supervisor.

There are several important considerations regarding planning and costs when implementing a virtual peer coaching innovation. Materials that are needed to implement the innovation include Skype software, Pamela Call Video Recording software, a computer or iPad, Bluetooth wireless USB adapter (for computer), Bluetooth headset (BIE), and a webcam. Excluding the costs associated with a personal computer and/or a tablet, the virtual peer coaching equipment and software costs approximately $80 per student for implementation, and the equipment is reusable.

In the beginning, the university provided the Bluetooth wireless USB adapter and headset at approximately $30 per student, which is less expensive than supervisor travel for face-to-face visits. With more and more candidates utilizing this technology, candidates are now required to purchase the Bluetooth headset. If students use an iPad, the USB adapter is not necessary because it is included in the iPad.

Still, the technology required to implement virtual coaching is much less than a textbook for most graduate classes. Supervising faculty need the Skype software, Pamela Call Video Recording software (if they plan to record the sessions), and a webcam (if their computer or mobile device does not have one).

The supervisors brainstormed a list of potential coaching prompts to be used during virtual coaching. Coaching prompts grounded in Bloom's Taxonomy were especially helpful and served as reminders to interns to ask higher-level questions during teaching and instruction. Incorporating suggestions to minimize distractions from Scheeler, Congdon, and Stansbery (2010), the supervisors utilized short phrases such as "Work the room," "Remember Bloom's," "Give wait time," "Stick with him," and "Avoid yes/no questions." Moreover, instructional behaviors characterized by the Danielson instrument framed coaching prompts that focused on planning and preparation, classroom environment (for example, fairness, rapport), and student engagement.

Typically, at this university, internship supervisors are assigned four interns per semester, equating to a three-credit-hour load. To be successful, the supervisors organized their observations well in advance of the semester. The convenience of the technology provided help early on when last-minute public school schedule changes allowed the supervisors to complete the BIE/Skype observations from work and home settings, thus reducing management and travel time. The supervisors unanimously reported that they experienced a more productive and efficient workload with virtual coaching than with previous face-to-face coaching (Benson and Cotabish, 2014).

BENEFITS OF VIRTUAL COACHING

The virtual peer coaching innovation utilized has already produced early positive benefits. In previous studies, Allen (2014) found virtual coaching to be helpful because it saves time and money, increases the number of observations for novice teachers, increases teaching effectiveness because of its immediate on-the-job feedback, and prevents isolation, which can be useful in decreasing the number of teacher dropouts.

In the virtual coaching internship experience described throughout this chapter, students demonstrated effective use of new technology, produced more thoughtful self-reflection essays, and immediately improved their teaching performance and instructional behaviors as a result of the on-demand corrective feedback. Similar results were found by Rock et al. (2009), reporting that 73 percent of teachers found the virtual peer coaching to be helpful and the program resulted in a significant improvement in instructional practices as well as increased student engagement.

Virtual coaching promotes a strong collaboration between the supervisor and intern, increasing the likelihood that student learning will be impacted. In the program described throughout this chapter, interns felt more connected to their supervisor through this model, as if they were partnering or co-teaching with their supervisor. In particular, interns reported positive and increased rapport with their supervisor due to the additional communication required to implement the innovation. One intern summed up this benefit, stating, "The frequent communication with my supervisor increased the personal nature of our professional relationship. I felt more comfortable about approaching her when I had questions or concerns regarding the internship experience."

Another reason for strong collaboration between the supervisor and intern (or mentor and mentee) could be the direct immediate feedback, not delayed after a lesson observation feedback, as in traditional coaching models. On-the-spot feedback is delivered during the teaching session by a coach who has expertise and is skilled in giving immediate feedback during task acquisition.

Sharplin, Stahl, and Kerhwald (2016) conducted a study with eight pre-service teachers using the Real Time Coaching Model. The Real Time Coaching Model involves virtual coaching during the lessons in which mentors offer prompts and guidance to help the pre-service teacher in real time as he or she teaches the lesson. These pre-service teachers reported experiencing significant improvements in their pedagogic practice, as they were able to identify skill gaps in a supportive way. They experienced improvements in their professional practice over the course of real-time coaching, concluding with more of a growth mindset (Dweck, 2014). Specific results of the Real Time Coaching Model included improved pedagogic practice, encouragement of goal development, and reflective practice. The experience was viewed as supportive, reducing stress in teaching, and emphasizing the value of immediate feedback (Sharplin Stahl, and Kerhwald, 2016).

Since using virtual coaching for intern supervision, all interns reported that they preferred the virtual supervision experience to the traditional, face-to-face supervision. Specifically, interns reported that virtual peer coaching was a more authentic experience, noting their students engaged in typical classroom behaviors and learning that was unfiltered and unaffected by an outside observer. They indicated the technology was convenient and increased their accessibility to the supervisor. Interns also shared that they were pleasantly surprised as to how well the technology worked during observations. To sum up their experience, one intern stated,

> I enjoyed this process. I thought it was helpful that we could get immediate input from our supervisor during the lesson using Skype. I can see how this can be a tool that can be used throughout a school district for teacher review and observations. I thought it was a less obtrusive way to conduct an observation. I also felt like students' behaviors were more honestly reflected during this type of observation versus having a guest in the room.

DISADVANTAGES OF VIRTUAL COACHING

Some disadvantages and limitations associated with the virtual peer coaching innovation have been identified. Owen (2015) found that virtual mentors must set boundaries and ensure that interactions did not build dependency and diminish the development of self-efficacy in their interns. Students can become overreliant on the virtual coach and lose self-confidence in their ability to think on their feet during teaching episodes.

Three primary disadvantages of virtual coaching include technology limitations within schools districts (for example, broadband Internet blocked, dropped Skype calls, and other Internet difficulties), the uncomfortable sense of *being intrusive* when supervisors provide immediate, on-demand feedback, and the loss of physical engagement due to the supervisor not being present in the classroom (aesthetics are missing).

Concerning technology limitations, it is difficult to work with school districts that are not equipped with broadband Internet, that block access to websites such as Skype, and have protocols in place that limit access to the Internet. Furthermore, outdated computer systems further escalate technical difficulties.

Coached teachers or interns can hear every word, murmur, and sigh from the supervisors or coaches during the observations. Supervisors should utilize the mute button to avoid unintentional feedback. It can be difficult to give appropriate feedback when instructional teaching is not going well, particularly when multiple comments are warranted. The interjection of multiple comments can feel intrusive and at times rude even though they are meant as constructive feedback. Last, supervisors may miss the face-to-face interactions in the classroom with both the intern and the K–12 population. There is something to be said for the university supervisor being present in the classroom, experiencing the school environment, and interacting with the children who are learning the lesson.

SUMMARY

Research has historically shown the importance of the internship experience during a teacher education program and the influence it has on future successful teaching. Virtual coaching offers a new and innovative way to provide more systematic feedback and bridge the miles from classroom setting to university offices where experts in the field work side by side with novice teachers to effect student learning.

Utilizing new and innovative technology to provide immediate feedback to teacher candidates is not only a significant improvement to teacher education programs, but shows early promise in increasing the instructional behaviors and student engagement of their benefactors. Specifically, on-demand feedback immediately redirects teaching behaviors before poor instructional practices have the opportunity to become poor instructional habits.

Key skills such as questioning and discussion techniques, student engagement, structure and pacing, monitoring of student learning, and feedback to students are important instructional behaviors and indicators of what beginning teachers should know. Virtual peer coaching has the potential to increase these target skills. Given the priority placed on improving student learning, increasing the frequency with which university supervisors provide corrective feedback is an important consideration in teacher education.

In terms of the financial impact, the innovation has the potential to decrease university travel budgets and/or allow the reallocation of travel funds to professional endeavors. With travel time diminished, faculty may have more control of their time management and scheduling, devoting more time to teaching, scholarship, and other relevant projects. The barrier of distance often encountered when traveling to remote schools is obsolete, further supporting programs utilizing online delivery formats.

As will be discussed in chapter 9, virtual peer coaching also has implications for K–12 school settings. Administrators can utilize the innovation for conducting classroom observations, instructional coaching, and for assessment purposes. Moreover, instructional coaches can use virtual peer coaching to provide on-demand feedback to redirect instructional behaviors.

The innovation may be an especially useful tool to assist teachers who have been placed on a professional improvement plan or require assistance with classroom management and student behavioral issues. Furthermore, on-demand corrective feedback can potentially increase levels of student engagement and promote teacher fairness among students as guidance is given in the moment by effective virtual coaches.

In summary, through virtual peer coaching a supervisor can provide support to a teacher without being physically present in the classroom and can observe authentic teacher and student interactions. Additionally, virtual peer coaching removes the barrier of distance and allows more teachers to receive the benefits and increased frequency of coaching interactions; however, these benefits do not come without a cost. Technology issues can be problematic and can limit the utilization of innovative tools such as these. Moreover, the supervisors experienced a fear of intrusiveness when using on-demand corrective feedback. However, as indicated by virtual coaching studies, the advantages of virtual peer coaching far outweigh the disadvantages.

QUESTIONS FOR REFLECTION

1. How can collaborative relationships between coaches and interns be enhanced through online formats?
2. What coaching prompts are most helpful to teachers in improving their instructional practices?
3. How could virtual coaching be utilized to enhance professional development and growth of practicing teachers?

Section III

Coaching Practicing Teachers

Section III focuses its attention on teachers in the classroom. The first chapter in this section discusses one university's efforts at bridging the gap between teacher candidate and practicing teacher. Faculty at this university volunteered to coach and mentor novice teachers as they engaged in their first year of teaching. The next chapter, chapter 7, highlights improvement of instructional practice through coaching elementary teachers as they implement a new science curriculum. In partnership with a local university, teachers work with coaches to effectively implement the curriculum. Following this chapter, integration of the arts into the curriculum is the target of the coaching relationship in chapter 8. Using peer coaching, teachers who engage in arts integration report increased understanding and ability to integrate as a direct result of their coaching experiences. The fourth chapter in this section (chapter 9) discusses embedded professional development through virtual coaching experiences. Suggestions and ideas for utilization of virtual coaching are presented and reviewed. Finally, there is the conclusion, which offers some ideas for initiating coaching and ends with questions for the reader to consider when stepping into the coaching realm.

Chapter Six

From Students to Teachers

University Faculty Coaching Novice Teachers

Donna Wake, EdD, and Victoria Groves-Scott, EdD, University of Central Arkansas

The challenges of beginning teachers have been a staple in the research and literature base for many years. The story of the young, idealistic teacher entering the classroom with aspirations to impact kids' lives and change the world are a common theme in literature and movies with notable exemplars including *Dangerous Minds*, *Dead Poet's Society*, *Freedom Writers*, and *To Sir with Love*.

These tales espouse the idea that if a teacher is committed enough, passionate enough, and selfless enough, he or she will make a lasting and notable impact on his or her students despite any bureaucratic blockades. Outside the context of Hollywood, research also documents the struggles of novice teachers beginning. As Sharon Feiman-Nemser (2012) writes,

> Lortie (1966) likened the new teacher to Robinson Crusoe, marooned on a desert island and facing the challenges of survival alone. In a more recent study, Johnson (2004) found that new teachers often feel lost at sea with little or no guidance from colleagues or curriculum. Despite changes in the backgrounds of teachers and the contexts of teaching, two themes persist: The early years of teaching are undeniably a time of intense learning, and they are often a time of intense loneliness. (p. 10)

A growing initiative in the education profession is the idea of induction support, that is, supporting beginning teachers as they enter the field by providing them with the resources and support to be successful and to create equitable and supportive classroom environments and instruction for all learners. Many of these induction programs are centered on professional development and coaching.

State departments of education and K–12 public schools have been working to support novice teachers for decades. However, the level of support novice teachers receive varies greatly and includes multiple formats, such as workshops, personal learning communities, and coaching from more experienced peers and administrators.

The effectiveness of this coaching is difficult to determine based on the different forms the coaching can take. Often teachers are arbitrarily paired with a veteran teacher and contact between the two is minimal, whereas other states and districts might train mentors and facilitate ongoing contact and support.

INDUCTION AND COACHING PROGRAMS

Induction and coaching programs have been present in the literature base since the mid-1980s, with evidence of the practice increasing in recent years. While only 40 percent of new teachers reported participating in an induction program in the early 1990s, more than 85 percent reported participating in induction programs in the early 2000s (National Center for Education Statistics [NCES], 2008).

The New Teacher Center (Goldrick et al., 2012) reported that more than half of states require new teachers to participate in some form of induction or coaching. While this increase can be viewed as positive, the quality and frequency of these induction experiences varies considerably with only a small percentage of new teachers experiencing high-quality, intensive induction.

More frequently, teachers report their professional development as lackluster or not responsive to their immediate needs (Lutrick and Szabo, 2012). Furthermore, the impact of much professional development (PD) offered to teachers is often vague, may not offer guidance for continued teacher development or school improvement, and may not support teachers in meeting students' needs. That being said, there is evidence to suggest that a combination of PD and follow-up support in the form of coaching can promote teacher effectiveness (Kretlow, Cooke, and Wood, 2012).

Induction and coaching programs have traditionally been the purview of state- or district-level initiatives. Despite the prevalence of state- and district-controlled models, there are a few exemplars of university-sponsored induction and/or programs and university and district collaborative programs focused on teacher induction (Gilles, Wilson, and Eaton, 2009).

The Comprehensive Teacher Induction Consortium has provided a model for university-based induction wherein universities collaborate with school/

district partners to provide induction support (Gilles, Wilson, and Eaton, 2009). Universities participating in this consortium include the University of Missouri, the University of Nebraska at Omaha, and Texas State University at San Marcos. These universities have collaborated to share information and have all based their induction programs on a model established at the University of New Mexico in cooperation with the Albuquerque Public Schools.

While these programs have some variation in implementation, they all share certain attributes, including (1) a full year of support and coaching from a carefully selected master teacher who also works closely with the university faculty, (2) coursework leading to a master's degree, (3) a cohort group, and (4) an action research capstone project.

The master teachers in this model have been released from their classroom duties in order to mentor new teachers (one-third of the time). They also assist in their schools on special projects (one-third of the time) and work with university faculty and candidates (one-third of the time).

The schools pay the salary of the master teacher and pay the university a fee equivalent to a midcareer teacher and receive two to three new teachers. The new teachers are paid a small stipend and their tuition and fees for a fifth-year master's degree are waived (Gilles, Wilson, and Eaton, 2009).

Results of these university-based induction programs are positive. Results include increased retention, increased teacher professional involvement, improved pedagogical practice, and significantly better pedagogical practice than noninduction-supported peers (Davis and Waite, 2006).

This chapter reports on an initiative by one education preparation provider (EPP) to support recent graduates in the form of university faculty mentorship/coaching while concurrently gathering the data required to meet accreditation expectations. Recent graduates of initial teacher licensure programs at one midsized, public university continued to work with faculty in a mentor-apprentice-coaching relationship.

Graduates and faculty were paired in the summer prior to the graduate's first year of full-time teaching. Graduates involved in the study volunteered to remain working with the EPP as a graduate cohort. Faculty coaching these graduates did so as a volunteer service project, and this resulted in additional work for these already busy faculty members.

We wish to use this chapter to describe an alternative to supporting novice teachers connected to university teacher education programs as a service-learning project. The study shares the experiences of novice teachers and university faculty. Early findings indicate that novice teachers can benefit from continued university support; however, the greater impact of the project was in informing university programs of their ability to prepare candidates for real-world contexts.

METHOD

Participants

Participants in the study included thirty-one novice teachers who all shared the attribute of graduating from the University of Central Arkansas College of Education teacher licensure programs in the 2015–2016 academic year. Participant attrition is an area of ongoing research. At the six-month mark, all thirty-one of the initial cohort had maintained at least the minimal level of contact with twelve of the sixteen participating graduates involved at a more substantial level. Subsequent cohorts may include a mix of graduates within their first one, two, and three years following graduation.

The initial cohort included eight graduates from the elementary licensure program, six graduates from the middle-level program, four graduates from the secondary programs (one science, one art, one social studies, one PE/health), and twelve graduates from the nontraditional Master of Arts in Teaching (MAT) program (two early childhood, five middle level, one secondary English, two science, one drama/speech, one business).

In December 2016, two additional middle-level licensure graduates joined the study, having graduated in December and immediately secured teaching positions in local schools. Consistent with research regarding teacher demographics (NCES, 2011), the study included twenty-seven females and five males; a median age of twenty-four; twenty-four Caucasians, four African Americans, one Asian American, and three graduates identifying as Other.

Convenience sampling was utilized. Subject randomization was not possible. According to the university's Institutional Research Board guidelines, teacher candidates participating in this study had to freely volunteer to participate. Participants were recruited from the 2015–2016 graduating class and the fall 2016 graduating class from all teacher education programs at the university. All participants were enrolled in the university's required internship course when they were offered the chance to be a part of this program.

The project also involved twenty-seven faculty participants who volunteered to take part in the project. It should be noted that some faculty involved in the project agreed to support two teachers. This faculty group included representation from all licensure programs as follows: four elementary/SPED, six MAT, ten middle level, two STEM, two secondary, and three other (that is, two deans and one faculty from leadership studies).

Faculty included nine tenured faculty, three tenure-track faculty, and fifteen clinical faculty. Faculty participants were recruited from the dean's office in multiple emails and meetings promoting the program and asking for volunteers. Additionally, a faculty committee was formed to oversee the design and implementation of the program. The committee included representation from all programs as follows: two elementary/SPED faculty, two MAT/middle-level faculty, and one secondary faculty.

Program Design

The faculty were determined that this initiative should rely on developing close, personal relationships with the graduates in order to ease their transition into the profession. The graduates were told that faculty merely wished to serve as a *critical friend* and to offer resources, a sympathetic ear, and an objective and external lens for the teachers' first-year experiences.

Whereas teachers may be reluctant to discuss issues with their school-based mentor for fear of judgment or of perceived weakness, an external faculty could serve as a safe harbor for discussions around the novice teachers' experiences. Additionally, many of these faculty had positive and preestablished relationships built on trust and previous experiences as graduates had taken classes with these faculty and/or been supervised by them in their student teaching.

A description of the study was presented to all candidates exiting teacher preparation internship. Participants then indicated interest by signing up on a provided Google Form. Beginning in July 2016, all 2015–2016 teacher education graduates also began receiving emails from the dean's office providing additional promotion of the programs, newly advertising two *back to school* workshops, and offering continued faculty support. These promotional activities resulted in additional enrollment in the program.

Graduates were paired with faculty based on personal preferences and licensure area. For example, a graduate working in a special education setting was matched with a faculty with a special education background. Graduates were informed that the program provided opportunities for continuous contact as needed through phone, email, text, and face-to-face visits both off and on school grounds.

In addition, faculty would visit the teachers' classrooms at least once to conduct informal observations and provide formative feedback. Graduates were also given information about structured workshops scheduled throughout the academic year that would also provide opportunity for networking in order to share resources, problem solve issues, and celebrate successes.

At each point of contact, potential participants were informed that a small grant had been secured to support the program that would provide them with a small stipend at the end of the 2016–2017 academic year if they entered the program, continued to be involved, and met minimal established guidelines. Additionally, all contact with faculty would be tracked and submitted to the state as earned professional development hours in addition to hours earned attending any of the provided workshops.

The committee overseeing this project met in September to formalize procedures for faculty and graduates around this project to ensure appropriate distribution of the stipend attached to this project. Faculty involved with this project also received a copy of the First-Year Teachers' Project Mentor Guidelines. This one-page document outlined the expectations for the participating teachers to include (1) sharing appropriate contact information with their faculty mentor, (2) engaging in communication with the mentor at least twice per month for PD hours using whatever method was most comfortable and convenient (for example, text, phone, face to face, email, etc.), (3) allowing mentors to visit classrooms for observations (alternatively observations could be conducted via various recommended technology options, such as bug in the ear,[1] video annotation), and (4) sharing contact information with the teacher's school-based mentor and school supervisor (for example, principal, curriculum head). All participants were invited to give input for revision of this document before it was finalized, and their input was used to modify some language in the guidelines.

The project coordinator reminded faculty and teachers of these requirements on a monthly basis. Faculty tracked contact hours and observation scores (based on the state observation rubric) through provided Google Form links. It should be noted that many faculty went above and beyond minimum expectations. These faculty visited their teachers' classrooms more than once, and some faculty even taught or co-taught in those classroom spaces, serving as a model for instructional practices.

To guide the observations, the state-adopted Teacher Excellence and Support System (TESS) model was used as the observation framework. All participants in the program were assessed using the TESS observation rubric.

The TESS rubric is based on Charlotte Danielson's (2007) *Enhancing Professional Practice: A Framework for Teaching*. The framework is a research-based protocol aligned to the Interstate New Teacher Assessment and Support Consortium (INTASC) standards and grounded in a constructivist view of teaching and learning that represents a consensus view of what a beginning teacher should know.

Finally, the faculty involved met several times over the course of the fall semester to compare notes and plan additional actions and will continue to meet as the project progresses.

FINDINGS

At the six-month point of program induction, statistics were gathered and evaluated to assess the health of the program and determine future direction. Data were analyzed from the two online data collection forms: The UCA First-Year Teacher Project Contact Log and the UCA First-Year Teacher

Project Teacher Observation Reporting Form. In addition, faculty involved in this project were invited to a meeting to discuss their experiences. Notes from this meeting were collected and analyzed.

UCA First-Year Teacher Project Contact Log

In the UCA First-Year Teacher Project Contact Log, seventy-five separate responses were logged of contact between faculty and new teacher. These contact points included twenty-seven of the thirty-one first-year teachers (90 percent) and twenty-four of the twenty-seven faculty (89 percent) involved in the project.

Participants and faculty logged seventy-one different contact points averaging at just over one hour (sixty-three minutes), with each point of contact ranging from thirty minutes to two hours. When broken down on a per-participant basis, faculty-teacher pairs spent on average over 2.6 hours in contact with each other over the fall semester (figure 6.1), with wide variation among faculty-teacher pairs' individual contact ranging from thirty minutes to 10.5 hours.

The recorded contact time between teachers and faculty in this project did indicate a continued need of the novice teachers for at least minimal levels of contact and support throughout the fall semester. While some novice teachers maintained only minimal or no contact, others showed a need for intensive and ongoing support and contact (figure 6.2).

Contact between faculty-teacher participant pairs was *led* by the novice teacher in terms of determining their preference and comfort. Contact between faculty and teachers occurred primarily via email (45.3 percent) and

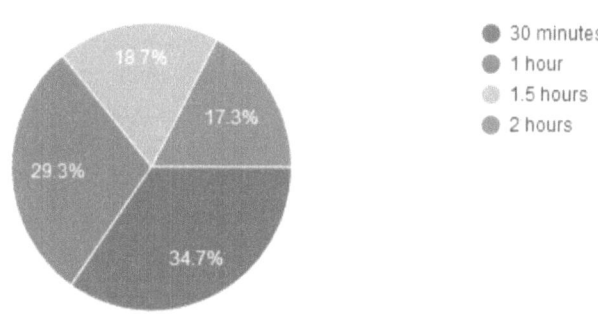

Figure 6.1. Faculty-Teacher Contact Hours

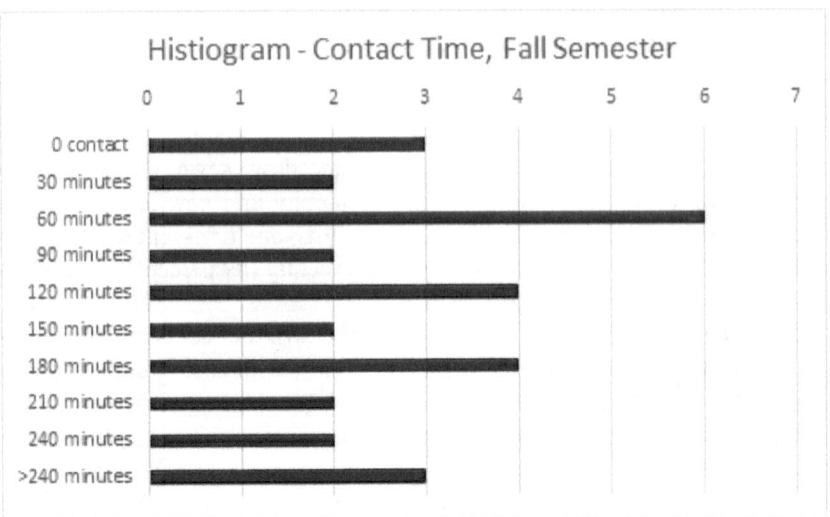

Figure 6.2. Amount of Contact Time with Novice Teachers

face-to-face contact (41.3 percent), followed by phone conversations (24 percent), text (16 percent), and Skype, Google Hangout, or FaceTime (6.7 percent) (figure 6.3). It should be noted that the percentage amounts to more than 100 percent in the data as faculty could select multiple options in recording any given contact over a minimum thirty-minute block of time.

When focusing on topics discussed during these points of contact, instructional strategies were favored (45.3 percent), followed closely by topics related to general classroom management related to managing student behavior (44 percent). Teachers also asked for guidance planning lessons (41.3 percent), support navigating professional aspects of their new job (36 percent), content-specific guidance (28 percent), and classroom management issues related to supporting instruction (for example, grouping, procedures, routines) (22.7 percent).

Finally, candidates asked for help in organization (for example, planning, preparing, record keeping) (10.7 percent) (figure 6.4). It should be noted that the percentage amounts to more than 100 percent in the data as faculty could select multiple options in recording any and all topics discussed with the novice teacher in a given point of contact.

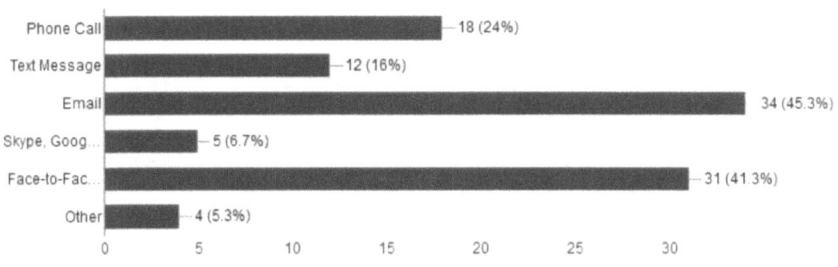

Figure 6.3. Mode of Contact with Novice Teachers

UCA First-Year Teacher Project Teacher Observation Reporting Form

Thirteen teacher observations were logged during the first semester of the project on eleven different graduates: three elementary, four middle level, three MAT, and one secondary. The framework divides the complex activity of teaching into twenty-two components (and seventy-six smaller elements) clustered into four domains of teaching responsibility.

The components are domain 1: planning and preparation, domain 2: classroom environment, domain 3: instruction, and domain 4: professional responsibilities. Each of the twenty-two components defines a distinct aspect of a domain; two to five elements describe each component, providing four levels of teaching performance describing each component as follows: *Unsatisfactory* (scored as a "1"), *Basic* (scored as a "2"), *Proficient* (scored as a "3"), and *Distinguished* (scored as a "4").

Graduates involved in this project scored highest in domain 4: professionalism (average 2.58 on a four-point scale), followed by domain 2: classroom management (average 2.53 on a four-point scale) and domain 1: planning and preparation (average 2.46 on a four-point scale). They scored lowest on domain 3: instructional strategies (average 2.43 on a four-point scale) (figure 6.5).

An examination of each of the twenty-two components yielded additional metrics to consider with graduate scores ranging from 2.07 to 3.17 (figure 6.6).

SUMMARY

The data tell us that early implementation of the university-based induction program is off to an uneven start. While the programs involved in this study

Topic(s) Discussed (75 responses)

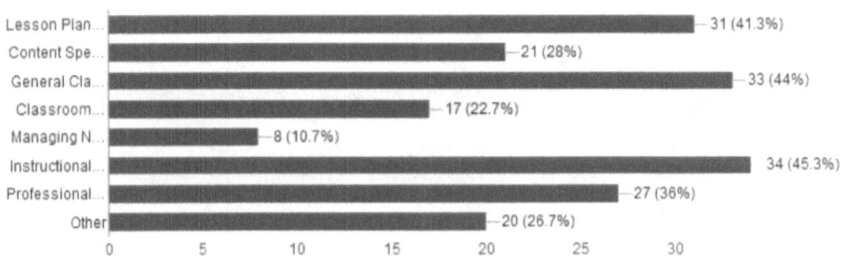

Figure 6.4. Topics Discussed during Coaching

graduated over four hundred teachers with initial licensure, only thirty-one teachers initially signed up for this induction experience, representing fewer than 10 percent of the targeted population.

While the intention of the faculty was to provide continuing and early support/coaching to novice teachers graduating from the programs, it appears that extending that support is not as easy as merely offering to remain connected in the role of a mentor/coach, even when a small stipend is offered to the participants.

Likewise, soliciting faculty input was also problematic with faculty from one department volunteering at a much higher rate than faculty from another department, causing some feelings of differential buy-in from the faculty stakeholders in the project despite assurances from the dean's office that this project was essential for continued accreditation.

IMPLICATIONS AND QUESTIONS

Given the experiences of the first six months of the induction project, it is clear that the model to support those teachers is one that needs further examination. The course-based model such as the ones offered at Missouri, Nebraska, and Texas may be warranted. The researchers and faculty question the impact of working more closely with Local Education Agencies (LEAs) to require or incentivize the program.

While the faculty involved in this project unselfishly offered their time and service gratis, this is a project that cannot be sustained given the energy required to sufficiently coach a new teacher. One other idea offered by the faculty involved in this project was to connect with retired teachers and university alumni to serve as the novice teacher mentors. In this way, faculty would not be directly involved, but the university could still support novice

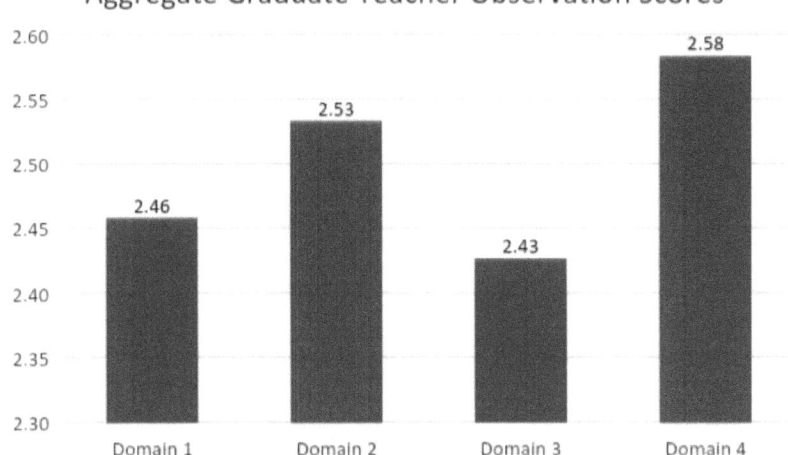

Figure 6.5. Novice Teacher Observation Scores

teachers and build a stronger *alumni and friends* chapter to support the mission of the College of Education.

Faculty recommendations for further project consideration also included developing coaching prompts and better training faculty involved in the project. For example, instead of coaches asking "How's it going," they could focus each week on asking "How is X going this week" and be more specific and intentional about conversations with the novice teachers. Additionally, faculty felt adding a social media component might drive up involvement by the novice teachers, particularly if they were highlighted and could share their successes with their colleagues.

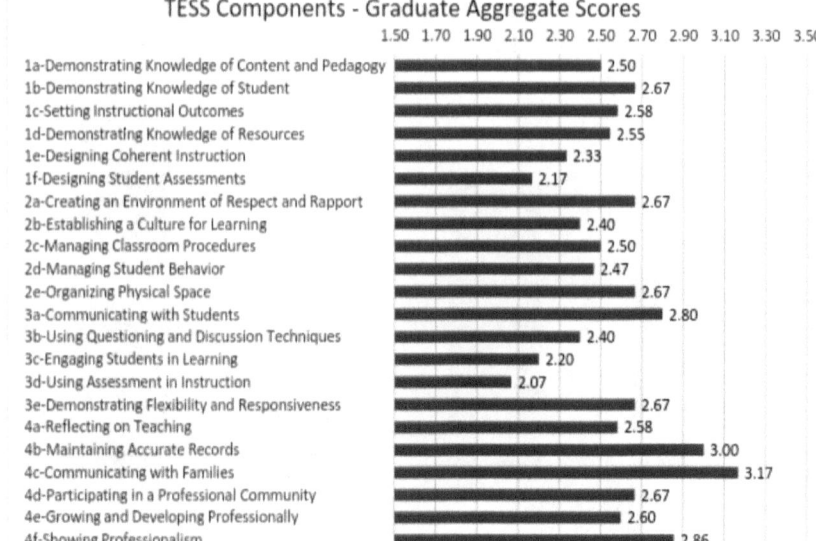

Figure 6.6.   Novice Teacher Observation Scores per Component

QUESTIONS FOR REFLECTION

1. What incentives could universities offer to encourage both graduates and education faculty to engage in a coaching model focused on a first-year induction program?
2. How could data generated from such a program be used to support continuous improvement efforts in teacher preparation programs, while simultaneously supporting first-year teacher growth and development?
3. What communication methods might be most successful in sustaining meaningful dialogue between first-year teachers and their faculty mentors?

NOTE

1. "Bug in the ear" refers to a Bluetooth device that is placed in the candidates' ear allowing the coach to provide constant feedback via the device in the moment. The device wirelessly receives aural input from a phone or tablet application, such as FaceTime, Skype, or Google Hangout. The coach can watch the classroom interactions via these applications with the device (with screen muted) positioned in the class background and provide comments to the teacher in real time. The coach gives prompts to guide the teacher to effective pedagogical practice and provides direct instruction promoting self-evaluation and prompting improved practice.

Chapter Seven

Coaching to Improve Teachers' Instructional Practices

Debbie Dailey, EdD,
University of Central Arkansas

Improving teachers' instructional practices is challenging and is rarely accomplished without embedded or extended support. Instructional coaching is an effective model used to provide teachers with embedded and extended support in their classroom. Positive effects include increased teacher content and pedagogical knowledge, self-efficacy for teaching, and improved student learning.

Effective coaching uses strategies such as modeling and facilitating classroom lessons, supporting teachers in content, and providing responsive feedback to facilitate instructional improvement. In particular, teachers proclaim that observing and talking to their coach is very beneficial for increasing their instructional knowledge and skills. For coaching to be effective, collegial rapport needs to be established early in the coaching relationship to enable sharing and collaborative learning. To maintain collegial rapport in the coaching dyad, the coach should not take on the role of *evaluator*, thus altering the relationship as a whole.

Effective coaches need good interpersonal skills and to be recognized as an expert in the content area, familiar with the operations of the classroom, and flexible when it comes to time. For example, one study found positive effects in the classroom when a connection was formed between the coach and teacher. The teacher recognized the competence of the coach, the coach provided instructional support, and the coach eased the teachers' isolation (Gustafson, Guilbert, and MacDonald, 2002).

This chapter will address types of coaching and will describe a coaching intervention. The coaching intervention will be evaluated through the effects on teachers and students. The chapter will conclude with practical applications and suggestions on how to implement coaching in a school. Questions of reflection are included to engage readers in formulating a coaching plan in their schools.

TYPES OF COACHING

Sweeney (2011) described three types of coaching: student-centered, teacher-centered, and relationship-driven coaching. Student-centered coaching is focused on changes at the student level. Student assessment data are used for instructional decision making and the coach provides instructional support as teachers move toward improving student learning.

On the other hand, teacher-centered coaching is focused on the teacher and how to improve his or her instructional practices. The coach supports the teacher in making instructional changes and uses student summative data to hold the teacher accountable. Finally, relationship-driven coaching is focused on the relationship between teacher and coach. The coach provides support through resources and materials in a nonthreatening way. Data is rarely used for decision making and the coach is seen as a resource to help achieve the goals of the program.

A COACHING INTERVENTION

Recently, a federally funded professional development intervention at the University of Arkansas at Little Rock was designed to prepare elementary teachers to implement a new science curriculum and improve their science teaching methods (Dailey and Robinson, 2016, 2017). Thirty teachers from two school districts participated in the study. A peer coach provided one-to-one professional development on an *as needed* basis.

During her school visits in the first year, the coach modeled effective science instruction, and as the teacher became more confident he or she assumed more of the science teaching responsibilities. During the second year, the coach continued her role as instructional facilitator supporting the teacher in areas of need. Outside of the classroom, she organized all necessary science activity materials and communicated with teachers in person or by phone or email to ensure their needs were being met.

During the first summer of the program, teachers attended a five-day summer institute emphasizing science content and pedagogy, specific problem-based curriculum units, classroom management, and technology.

During this institute, teachers actively engaged in the lessons from the science units by assuming the role of students. Teachers indicated that they appreciated the opportunity to actively participate in the lesson activities prior to enacting the lessons in their classrooms. They commented that being able to complete the activities and experiments that would be used in their own classrooms provided them with the perspective of the student and enhanced their own understanding. Teachers indicated that they valued the specific training on their classroom-based curriculum, a professional development strategy found to improve instructional practices.

During the second year of the project, the summer institute was responsive to teacher needs. Teachers requested additional training on the curriculum units, strategies to assist with managing a science classroom, and additional technology resources to engage students in learning. To this regard, teachers again actively participated in the professional development, taking the role of students. Instructional coaching actually began in the summer institutes in which teachers and the coach engaged in collaborative conversations detailing how to best assist them as they implemented the new curriculum.

The collegial relationship between coach and each teacher was established early on and solidified during the first school year. Revisiting Sweeney's (2011) descriptions of coaching methods, the coach implemented a combination of student-centered coaching and relationship-driven coaching. The focus was on designing appropriate instruction to improve student learning. Data were used to evaluate the effectiveness of the program but not the effectiveness of the teacher or students' progress toward mastery of the objectives.

Emphasis was placed on relationship building between the coach and each teacher. Because many teachers had little experience in teaching science, the coach often provided instructional support through modeling or facilitating the teacher with instruction, offered constructive feedback and suggestions for improvement, and provided multiple materials and other resources to assist teachers in their classrooms.

The coach was not considered an evaluator but more of an assistant and a resource, and eventually a friend. Initially, teachers were hesitant about the coach's presence in their classrooms, but soon realized that she could be valuable to them as they implemented the new science curriculum. In fact, during her last week, many teachers handed the coach notes and small tokens of appreciation.

On the external evaluator report, teachers praised the peer coaching intervention as being instrumental to positive changes in their instruction and classroom. They also praised the support and collegiality of the coach and referred to her as a human Xanax because of her encouragement and positive leadership.

EFFECTIVENESS OF A COACHING INTERVENTION

A conceptual framework was designed to guide this professional development program highlighting the necessary components needed to improve elementary science instruction (figure 7.1).

To enact and sustain change in elementary science classrooms, professional development (coaching in summer institutes and classrooms) addressed the common barriers to science instruction (time constraints, science teaching resources, teachers' science knowledge and skills, and science teaching confidence), focused on specific classroom practices and content, utilized a strong curriculum, provided sustained and follow-up support, and involved collective participation of teachers.

As guided by the conceptual framework (figure 7.1), the professional development sought to improve teachers' instructional practices, science content knowledge and skills, and science teaching confidence, perceptions, and self-efficacy. In response to teacher changes, the conceptual framework predicted students would exhibit positive effects in science knowledge and skills.

As suggested by Guskey (1986), when teachers realized the impact on students, they were encouraged to continue the innovation or program, thus increasing their confidence and self-efficacy for teaching science. Accordingly, the conceptual framework integrated the dependency of both the teach-

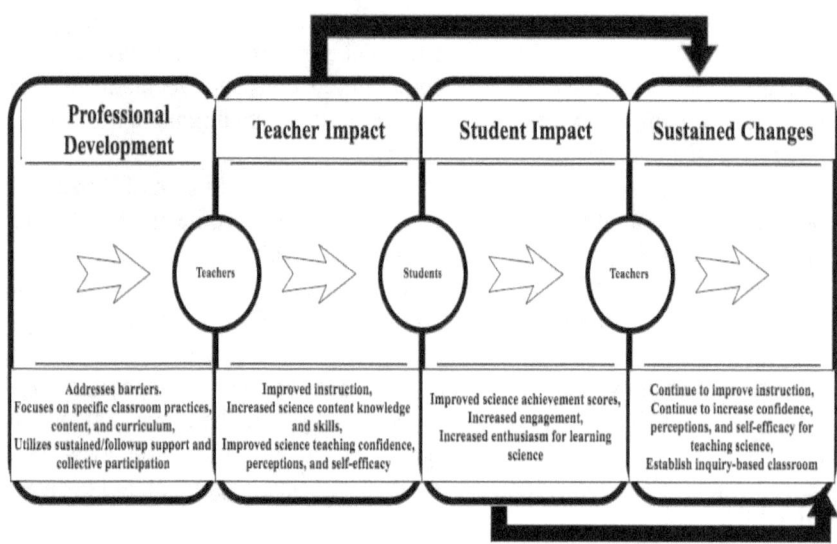

Figure 7.1. Conceptual Framework: Blueprint to Enact Sustained Changes in Elementary Science

er and the student on sustained changes in the participating elementary science classrooms.

IMPACT ON TEACHERS

In comparison with a control group, the professional development team found that teachers exhibited improvement in science teaching perceptions and science process skills, and these were sustained at least one year past the intervention.

In particular, teachers demonstrated increased perceptions in regard to questions such as, "I am confident in my foundational knowledge of the science content I teach," "I provide opportunities for students to design experiments based on their own questions about science," "My students generate their own concepts and ideas about scientific information after conducting an investigation," and "My students discuss science concepts from multiple perspectives."

In addition, participating teachers increased their scores on a measure of science process skills (Diet Cola Test: tests the ability to design an experiment) and sustained these scores one year past the intervention.

Through interview data, the participating teachers indicated that the professional development intervention, their increased frequency in teaching science, and their students' enthusiastic responses to the curriculum served to bolster their self-confidence in teaching science. Specifically, teachers attributed the changes to their instruction to the support received from coaching and the modeling of effective instruction.

In the external evaluator report, teachers provided descriptions of the coach: "[she] is a gem, she is in touch with teachers and science, just being out of the classroom herself, the students also relate well to her"; "[she] has been wonderful by helping with experiments, providing support, modeling lessons, being positive, providing websites and other resources, and engaging them in open communication weekly."

IMPACT ON STUDENTS

The ultimate test of a professional development program is the effect on students. After all, student learning is the basis for improving classroom instruction. In comparison to a control group, students in participating classrooms demonstrated statistically significant increases from pre- to post-test on measures of science content and concept knowledge and experimental design.

On a more informal note, the engagement, excitement, and buy-in from students was palpable. Students eagerly awaited the coach's visits to their classroom because they knew they would *do science* that day. Students would exclaim "our scientist is here" in regard to her arrival.

One day the coach received a text from a participating second-grade teacher. The second-grade unit focused on weather and the class had spent many weeks designing a weather garden, collecting and analyzing weather data, and learning about the causes of changes in weather. During recess on a very cloudy, windy, and sticky day, second-grade students approached the duty teacher and told her that there must be a change in weather coming because of the wind and the humidity and that a low-pressure system was approaching. For students to recognize changes in weather and the possible causes is exciting, but for them to discuss it at recess is evidence of student buy-in.

Clearly, this combination of teacher professional development employing coaching in summer institutes and in teachers' classrooms, as well as quality curriculum, positively impacted teachers' instruction and thereby promoted student learning in science.

SUMMARY

The professional development described in this chapter utilized expert coaching. The coach was a former high school science teacher with additional experience in providing professional development to teachers. She had also recently worked in elementary schools as a gifted and talented teacher. This program was funded by a multimillion-dollar federal grant that financially supported the coach, provided materials to classrooms, and awarded teachers stipends for participation.

Teachers' schedules are demanding and they need compensating if we ask for additional time beyond the school day. Consequently, programs such as the one described here are expensive to implement and therefore not always feasible for many school districts.

Other options schools could consider are using their science specialists or high school science teachers as coaches or using peer teachers as reciprocal coaches. Reciprocal coaches alternately observe, provide feedback, and engage with each other in collaborative discussions about their teaching. Additionally and as described in this book, alternatives to observing classrooms in person include using virtual technologies to observe teachers without being present in the classroom. Bug in the ear technology and Skype allow observation and feedback in real time, thereby addressing positive or negative instruction as it is occurring.

Applications such as VideoAnt (annotated video) improve the feedback associated with observing teachers using videos. Although the observation is not in real time, feedback can be time stamped so that observers can pinpoint the time at which a behavior occurs. Regardless of the type of coaching, engaging teachers in collaborative relationships in which they can share their expertise, provide feedback, and observe effective teaching is beneficial to promoting instructional improvement and therefore student learning.

QUESTIONS FOR REFLECTION

1. What do you consider the most valuable tool in coaching? Is it feedback, reflection, observation, modeling, etc.? Support your answers with research evidence.
2. How could you design a peer coaching intervention on a minimal budget? What resources could you utilize that are at your disposal?
3. How could you encourage a teacher to participate in a coaching program who is resistant to change?
4. Develop a proposal to submit to your administrator requesting a coaching intervention for teachers in your schools. The plan could be focused on areas of concern, such as content, classroom management, and pedagogy. Include suggestions for coaching dyads, types of coaching to be used, and a model of how coaching could change classroom practices.

Chapter Eight

Coaching for Arts Integration

Arkansas A+

Rachelle Miller, PhD,
University of Central Arkansas

Although standardized tests have become the measuring stick for student and school success, this may not be the most appropriate method to evaluate academic achievement. As President Obama stated at a town hall event in 2011, "One thing I never want to see happen is schools that are just teaching to the test. . . . [The students in those schools] are not learning about science, they're not learning about math. . . . Young people do well in stuff they're interested in. They're not going to do as well if it's boring" (as cited in Kain, 2011, para. 5).

Standardized tests provide valid and reliable ways to evaluate academic achievement, but other methods, such as performance assessments, can also accurately measure the academic growth and progress of students. Due to the current requirements of accountability and standards, schools are pressured to demonstrate continuous growth in student performance and use programs that will support these improvements.

Students who are from low-income families face the most challenges in enhancing academic achievement. Integrating the arts into the curriculum can possibly increase the levels of student engagement, participation, and achievement of students from various socioeconomic backgrounds.

ARTS INTEGRATION

According to Silverstein and Layne (2014), "Arts integration is an approach to teaching in which students construct and demonstrate understanding through an art form. Students engage in a creative process which connects an art form and another subject area(s) and meets evolving objectives in both" (para. 1).

Arts integration provides various benefits for students, including increased engagement levels, cognitive growth, long-term memory, creativity, and social skills; varied classroom activities to engage students; and reduced student stress (Sousa and Pilecki, 2013).

More specifically, students' long-term memory can be improved through the use of arts integration when students are doing the following tasks: (1) rehearsing information and skills, (2) interpreting content through the use of art, (3) creating information through artistic avenues, (4) performing dramatic presentations of content, (5) sharing information orally, (6) providing effort when creating meaning, (7) connecting emotions to content, and (8) using visuals to present information. Throughout this process students can be given opportunities to evaluate and create content, which would allow them to work at the highest levels of Bloom's Taxonomy.

Arts integration can "introduce and create enthusiasm for a new unit of study; reinforce concepts already learned; and enrich current content by adding another layer of meaning" (Lynch, 2007, p. 34). This chapter will provide a description of Arkansas A+ Schools, peer coaching in one A+ School, and ways to provide peer coaching if your school is not an A+ School.

ARKANSAS A+ SCHOOLS

The Arkansas A+ Model places an emphasis on arts integration, along with seven other components that all focus on engaging the learner in a student-centered classroom. Arts integration is woven throughout all of the components. The arts are integrated into the various content areas and include drama, dance, music, visual art, and writing.

These eight components are identified as the A+ Essentials, which include the following: instruction in the arts, thematic and interdisciplinary curriculum mapping and design (to include the arts), a focus on experiential learning, planning instruction for multiple learning pathways, enriched assessment design, collaborative classroom design, a supportive school infrastructure, and a climate of teacher autonomy.

Once a school becomes identified as an A+ School, teachers participate in professional development (PD) for three consecutive years and receive funding in order to support their implementation of the eight A+ Essentials. Prior to year one of implementation, teachers participate in a five-day summer institute, which introduces them to the eight essentials and various arts-integrated activities and resources.

During the second and third years, teachers receive two days of PD each summer and are also provided a one-day PD during the fall and spring semester. The PD during years two and three is more heavily focused on curriculum development specific to teachers' content area(s) and grade level(s). All PD sessions are conducted by arts specialists and/or A+ fellows. A+ fellows are individuals who have been trained in the A+ Essentials and who are working/retired teachers or teaching artists.

CHANGING EDUCATION THROUGH THE ARTS (CETA)

For the past three years, the author and her colleagues have completed program evaluation for Arkansas A+ Schools. All of the program suggestions provided to the executive director were based on the data collected from teachers in currently established Arkansas A+ Schools.

One of the suggestions was to create a peer coaching project that was a modified version of the Changing Education through the Arts (CETA) Model Schools program (John F. Kennedy Center for Performing Arts, 2008). Researchers have indicated that the CETA Model has positively influenced teachers' perceptions and attitudes about arts integration.

In addition, students' engagement and retention of content improved through the use of this model (Isenberg et al., 2009). Key features that are similar across the CETA Model Schools program and Arkansas A+ Schools' peer coaching are the use of an arts specialist and the structure of the coaching sessions.

However, there are several components that are unique to the Arkansas A+ peer coaching project, such as the following:

- Teachers worked closely with an arts specialist *and* an A+ fellow. (*The arts specialist was an art education professor from a local university. Two A+ fellows were part of this project and both were retired teachers.*)
- There were sixteen (nine lesson-planning sessions, seven teaching sessions) classroom peer coaching sessions instead of five proposed by the CETA Model Schools program.
- Professional learning communities (PLCs) were scheduled to occur throughout the course of the project. During every teaching session, the remaining teachers in the same grade level would observe each arts-integrated lesson. After the lesson, all teachers in that grade level along with the A+ fellow and arts specialist would debrief about the lesson. (*This was initially proposed to occur, but because of logistical constraints during the project, teachers were not able to observe one another and PLCs were not able to be conducted.*)

Chapter 8
ARKANSAS A+ PEER COACHING

After the first year of implementing the Arkansas A+ Model in three schools, teacher focus groups were conducted to gain a better understanding of teachers' perceptions and concerns about participating in the A+ program. Teachers were asked to describe their experiences, challenges/barriers, A+ activities, additional support/resources, and overall feelings about the A+ Model.

Teacher responses were grouped into the following major themes: the perceived benefits teachers saw from the A+ Model program implementation, the barriers and challenges they experienced, teacher requests for specific support and resources, and teacher perceptions of how the model helped and/or hindered them in their instructional practice.

Teacher perception at all three sites was primarily positive even though teachers acknowledged some barriers and challenges and made requests of the A+ program for additional support. The school whose teachers requested the most additional support was chosen to participate in the peer coaching project.

One particular school, Madison Elementary (pseudonym), acknowledged the most challenges and barriers and requested the most support from Arkansas A+ Schools. A peer coaching project was proposed in order to meet this particular school's need. During January 2016, a peer coaching project at Madison Elementary began. Two Arkansas A+ fellows and an arts education professor partnered with six teachers in grades K–5. One teacher at each grade level took the lead to work with one of the fellows and an arts education professor over the course of eight weeks.

Week one was devoted to planning and goal setting using the Arkansas A+ Essentials. The fellows and arts education professor planned and modeled lessons during weeks two and three. Lessons were co-planned and co-taught with the classroom teacher during weeks four and five. During weeks six through eight, the classroom teacher independently planned and taught the arts-integrated lessons and the A+ fellow was in the classroom for assistance.

Between sessions, the fellows were readily available via email and by phone in case the teacher needed additional help. This plan was modified and adjusted depending on the needs of each individual teacher. After each lesson, the fellow and teacher debriefed the lesson to discuss the various A+ Essentials that were used throughout the lesson. Throughout the project, data were gathered through teacher observations, teacher interviews, and a survey.

TEACHER OBSERVATIONS

Teacher observations were completed before peer coaching (time 1), at the end of peer coaching (time 2), and two months after peer coaching (time 3). Teachers were evaluated with the A+ Teacher Observation Protocol (A+TOP; Miller, Wake, and Whittingham, 2015) during each time period. The A+TOP targets teacher behaviors associated with the eight essentials of the A+ Program. The A+TOP was developed directly from the stated A+ Model and curriculum progressions and includes eight criteria and four levels of performance (1 = *No Evidence*, 2 = *Basic*, 3 = *Proficient*, and 4 = *Distinguished*).

Prior to the peer coaching project, all six teachers showed "No Evidence" in all essentials except critical thinking. Teachers demonstrated "Critical Thinking" at the "Basic" level. Teachers showed an increase in all essentials at the end of the peer coaching project: arts (1.80), curriculum (1.67), assessment (1.28), experiential learning (0.90), multiple learning pathways (1.73), critical thinking (0.83), collaboration (1.20), and climate (1.05). Teachers demonstrated the greatest growth in the arts integration essential. Teachers showed "Basic" and "Proficient" scores in all essentials at the end of the peer coaching session (time 2).

In order to evaluate sustainability, teachers were observed again two months after the peer coaching project. Although they demonstrated lower scores in time 3, their scores were still higher than time 1 in seven of the eight essentials: arts, curriculum, assessment, experiential learning, multiple learning pathways, critical thinking, and climate.

During time 3, teachers showed "No Evidence" to some evidence in four of the essentials (that is, arts, curriculum, collaboration, climate) and "Basic" in the remaining four essentials (that is, assessment, experiential learning, multiple learning pathways, critical thinking). Table 8.1 includes teachers' performance on the A+ Essentials before and after the peer coaching project.

TEACHER INTERVIEWS

Teachers were interviewed at the end of their peer coaching experience. The following topics were discussed during the interview: co-teaching experiences, A+ fellow and arts specialist, challenges/barriers, A+ Essentials, sample arts-integrated lessons, and additional support/resources. The following themes were prevalent in teachers' responses:

- Teachers greatly appreciated the experience working one-on-one with the A+ fellows and arts specialist. Even after teaching for twenty-two years, one teacher stated that it felt like "having your own personal trainer." She

Table 8.1. Madison Teachers' Scores on the A+TOP

Criteria	Before peer coaching (Time 1)	At the end of peer coaching (Time 2)	Two months after peer coaching (Time 3)
Arts	1.20	3.00	1.80
Curriculum	1.00	2.67	1.40
Assessment	1.80	3.08	2.20
Experiential Learning	1.60	2.50	2.20
Multiple Learning Pathways	1.60	3.33	2.60
Critical Thinking	2.00	2.83	2.20
Collaboration	1.80	3.00	1.80
Climate	1.20	2.25	1.90

recommended that every teacher should experience having a peer coach because she learned so much over the course of the eight weeks.
- Teachers gained a better understanding of how to effectively integrate the arts into their curriculum.
- Arts specialists and fellows provided a plethora of resources and modeled how to plan and implement an arts-integrated lesson.
- There are current obstacles with infrastructure that make it difficult to collaborate with the music and arts specialist at their school. Teachers' common planning time occurs when students go to art or music class.
- Teachers from the peer coaching project felt like they were more equipped to assist their colleagues with the implementation of the A+ Essentials.
- Teachers would like to have continued support from the A+ fellows. One teacher asked if the A+ fellows could visit them once a month to further assist them with arts integration and interdisciplinary curriculum design.

TEACHER SURVEY

The Content and Construct Development of the PACT Survey (Miller, Wake, and Whittingham, 2016) was used to examine how much teachers valued arts integration, their willingness to integrate the arts into the lessons, and the barriers they felt may inhibit them from integrating the arts. The survey consists of thirty-five questions on a five-point scale (that is, 1 = *strongly disagree*, 2 = *disagree*, 3 = *neutral*, 4 = *agree*, 5 = *strongly agree*). Teachers completed this survey before and after the peer coaching project.

After the eight-week peer coaching project, teachers *valued* arts integration more (0.23 increase), were more *willing* to integrate the arts into their lessons (0.84 increase), and perceived fewer *barriers* about integrating the arts (1.02 decrease). The means for the pre- and post-scores are included in table 8.2.

RECOMMENDATIONS FOR FUTURE SUPPORT OF A+ PEER COACHING

A+ teachers continue to be passionate about arts integration, even more so after the peer coaching project. However, teachers need continued and consistent support from an A+ fellow and an arts specialist. The following recommendations are provided for future support of Arkansas A+ teachers and also for administrators and/or teachers who are interested in collaborating with their staff in order to integrate the arts:

- If funding would permit, schools should consider hiring a full-time A+ fellow (that is, arts integration specialist) who would be part of the school's faculty. The fellow could then provide
  - peer coaching for the entire faculty,
  - assistance during teachers' common planning time,
  - PLCs at each grade level,
  - resources for teachers, and
  - opportunities to brainstorm with the art and music specialist for classroom integration ideas.
- Focus heavily on creating an exemplar A+ School.
  - Create a climate so that the entire school "feels" like an A+ School. One would completely be immersed in art as you walk through the hallways and classrooms. The arts would be regularly integrated into various content areas and through the use of various art domains.
  - A full-time A+ fellow would be part of the school's faculty, similar to a math or reading specialist.
  - This school would become the "shining star" for A+ Schools.
  - Create videos of arts-integrated lessons. (This began with the peer coaching project.)

Table 8.2. Means of Pre-/Post-PACT Survey

	Value	Willingness	Barriers
Pre ($n = 6$)	4.27	3.66	3.35
Post ($n = 2$)	4.50	4.50	2.33

- Create a curriculum library of various arts-integrated resources. (This started with the peer coaching project.)

• Provide course offerings or workshops so that teachers can learn about ways to integrate their curriculum with specific art domains.

  - There appears to still be a disconnect, misunderstanding, or maybe just lack of knowledge in the arts, so teachers do not seem fully equipped to implement true arts integration. Even after peer coaching, teachers perceived that they were integrating the arts into their lessons, but it was not at the level that was used during the peer coaching sessions.

• Participate in common planning time with the arts specialist.

  - Teachers and the arts specialist can discuss ways that the arts could be integrated into their curriculum or ways that they could integrate a content area(s) into the art curriculum. This could lead to co-teaching opportunities during art class or general classroom.

MODIFIED VERSION OF A+ PEER COACHING

The remainder of this chapter describes how five teachers integrated the arts in a summer camp with help from an arts specialist (peer coach).

During the summer of 2016, five practicing teachers completed their practicum for their Gifted and Talented Education endorsement at the University of Central Arkansas. Their practicum consisted of creating a STEAM unit and teaching it in STEMulate Engineering Academy—a four-day summer engineering camp for gifted students in grades three through five. Two teachers co-taught each STEAM unit.

Prior to STEMulate Engineering Academy, the teachers shared their completed engineering units with an arts specialist. The arts specialist reviewed each unit and noted various ways that the arts could be integrated into the curriculum, based on Silverstein and Layne's (2014) definition of arts integration.

The arts specialist suggested ways to integrate visual arts into the teachers' unit and provided resources to help teachers and students gain a deeper understanding of art content. Teachers reviewed the arts specialist's notes, and then each pair of teachers met with the arts specialist one-on-one for approximately one hour. The arts specialist discussed her notes in detail and taught the teachers several basic art concepts that could be integrated into the lesson. She also provided them with the necessary resources in order to teach in depth about each art concept and connect it to engineering concepts.

At the end of STEMulate Engineering Academy, teachers were interviewed to discuss their experiences teaching a STEAM unit. Teachers also completed the PACT Survey, which examined their perceptions about arts integration. Interview responses indicated that teachers believed that they gained a comprehensive understanding of arts integration, and they felt like they grew professionally during this process.

In addition, teachers discussed that students were engaged and had a deeper understanding of the content throughout this process. Survey results indicated that teachers' value of arts integration remained high through the study. After teaching a STEAM unit, teachers were less willing to integrate the arts, but also felt that there were fewer barriers. Because they only received one hour of PD, they still lacked the self-efficacy to create and teach lessons on their own, suggesting that opportunities to co-teach with an arts specialist would be beneficial, in addition to participating in more art content PD.

If someone is interested in beginning an arts integration peer coaching project on a smaller scale like the one described here, one suggestion would be to begin an ongoing collaboration with one or more arts specialists. Samples of high-quality, arts-integrated lessons that incorporate various art domains are at the Kennedy Center for Performing Arts: https://artsedge.kennedy-center.org/educators/lessons.

SUMMARY

Arts integration increases the level of student engagement and provides a deeper understanding of content. Collaborating with an arts specialist through peer coaching could occur on a larger whole-school scale like Arkansas A+ Schools or on a smaller scale by working one-on-one with an arts specialist at one's school. The key component is that peer coaching should be an ongoing process until the teacher feels like he or she can confidently create and teach arts-integrated lessons on his or her own.

QUESTIONS FOR REFLECTION

1. Reflect on the two peer coaching projects in this chapter. Which one would be more feasible at your school? What are some modifications that may have to occur?
2. There are various benefits to interdisciplinary lessons, such as increasing student engagement and providing a deeper understanding of content. What type(s) of support do you think teachers need in order to create more interdisciplinary opportunities for their students?

Chapter Nine

Embedded Professional Development

Virtually Coaching Classroom Teachers

Nykela Jackson, PhD,
University of Central Arkansas

Education reform has and continues to be a debatable topic. Challenges such as low student test scores, limited funding, teacher shortages, low teacher pay, overcrowded classrooms, bullying, lack of parental involvement, and students' lack of respect for teachers are at the forefront of most educational policy and school improvement discussions. Establishing a plan to tackle these issues is easier said than done. Lawmakers, educators, parents, and students offer varying recommendations and opinions on how to solve these crises. Because there are no clear-cut answers, one method that has been confirmed to enhance school improvement is teacher quality.

Teacher quality (for example, impressive pedagogy, commitment to student learning, knowledge of content, effective management, clear feedback, reflection on teaching) has a direct influence on student learning, which impacts the overall school environment. The most powerful way to affect teacher quality, which directly impacts student achievement, is through sustained professional development.

Teachers need ongoing professional development and support to successfully navigate the pervasive issues found in today's classrooms. However, professional development (for example, workshops, courses, content materials, conferences) alone is not enough to reflect improvement. Key factors in professional development include application of learning in the classroom and continuous support. Collaboration, coaching, follow-up support, and explicit instruction impact teaching practices.

Sustained support, in addition to quality and accessibility, is critical for effective professional development. One challenge schools face is affordability, as intense and frequent professional development can be costly for school districts (for example, time away from classroom, paid substitutes, required resources for implementation, travel from rural locations). Although most schools have reduced the amount of traditional professional development offered and have invested more in online professional development, the classic one-size-fits-all solution seldom provides the needed benefits for individualized improvement and application during the school year.

One proposed solution to these problems is virtual coaching (real-time coaching through a videoconferencing format), which can be used as a professional development tool by facilitating peer coaching in schools and across districts.

PROFESSIONAL DEVELOPMENT DELIVERY SYSTEMS

The goal of professional development is to improve classroom instruction, which correlates to student advancement. Quality professional development offers teachers a chance to actively engage in learning through collaboration, inquiry, application, and reflection. Through collaboration, teachers can discuss teaching and learning strategies with other professionals and analyze their successes and shortcomings.

Inquiry leads to more in-depth investigation of these deficiencies and identification of new strategies that can meet the teachers' needs. Application provides the opportunity to try recommended methods to determine their effects. Lastly, reflection extends learning by identifying additional targets for improvement and creating feedback on the sustainability of effective strategies.

Most professional development programs (traditional and online) offer collaboration, inquiry, and application, but do not offer reflection through real-time and immediate feedback. Virtual coaching supplies the chance for teachers to receive feedback while teaching and debriefing with a coach (for example, colleague, administrator, professional development leader) to reflect on professional practice and clarify current methods after the lesson.

Traditional professional development is typically delivered through a workshop or conference. Teachers attend training to sit and get new information and strategies to try in their classrooms. Another method used is a face-to-face observation, in which the teacher is evaluated using some type of scoring method and receives feedback following the examination. This application-based process allows the teacher to employ new strategies, receive outsider feedback, and recognize target areas for improvement. Although the constructive criticism is delayed, teachers can discuss the feedback, learn from mistakes, and have adequate time to make changes.

Online professional development is similar to traditional, except information is presented in a virtual format. The objective of providing new or enhanced information to help teachers become more effective is the same; the main difference is the delivery method. Online professional development offers the additional convenience of being more cost effective and convenient for teachers and school districts. Regardless of the setup (synchronous or asynchronous), teachers can engage in discussion and collaborate with others. In addition, videoed lessons can be watched and analyzed at a more suitable time for the observer.

Teachers benefit from both traditional and online professional development. Why should schools invest time and resources for virtual coaching? Virtual coaching encompasses both modalities; it allows teachers to obtain feedback during real-time instruction. Coaches or supervisors use bug in the ear technology (webcam and videoconferencing) to communicate directly with the teacher to share knowledge, suggestions, ideas, and support while the lesson is being taught. The teacher is coached through challenging situations, provided with interventions, or informed of missed opportunities as these situations arise.

The immediate feedback from virtual coaching directly benefits novice teachers to help navigate classroom confrontations instead of offering postponed suggestions after the fact. These prompt recommendations also assist seasoned teachers as they apply new strategies and refine current practices.

THE CULTURE OF VIRTUAL COACHING

Schools and teachers pursue professional development opportunities that are specific to their needs. Teachers who participate in training are expected to take what they learned and implement it into the classroom. Regardless if teachers are excited about the professional development or not, oftentimes they fall short during the application phase. The new information ends up collecting dust on a shelf or it is postponed until after state testing is completed at the end of the year. Pursuing the next step to apply what was learned in the classroom is not embraced due to lack of support.

While the trainer may have done an excellent job facilitating the professional development, demonstrating its importance, and allowing the teachers to practice the strategies during the workshop, when there is no direction and guidance once teachers get back to their classrooms, they may struggle with transferring the skills. Virtual coaching expands the application step by providing teachers the chance to practice what they learned and receive real-time feedback from a colleague.

Coaching promotes self-evaluation and reflection in pursuit of continuous improvement. Effective teachers seek recommendations and guidance on how to improve instruction and performance. Through collaboration, support, and feedback, virtual coaching allows a critical friend to observe instruction in a nonjudgmental way. Whether a content area expert or a peer colleague, the coach's objective is to observe, guide, and offer support to enhance classroom practice. A learning agenda and clear protocol are established to direct focus on the teacher's needs. The coach or critical friend understands the target for professional development and works with the teacher to achieve his or her desired goals.

Virtual coaching can be used for a variety of purposes to enhance teacher quality. For intervention purposes, schools can use virtual coaching to pair novice and/or struggling teachers with exemplary teachers to work on specific areas of improvement. Administrators can use this professional development avenue to mediate issues with teachers who received negative reviews. This process can be used as a form of enrichment for veteran teachers who have effective instruction but want to try out new strategies.

It can also be used to rectify specialty teacher isolation (for example, gifted, special education, music, art) or in small schools that have limited numbers of teachers. Because teachers usually have a restricted number of colleagues who teach similar content in their schools, virtual coaching can be used to build community and utilize professional colleagues who teach similar content outside of the school. This inexpensive and accessible approach provides flexibility for teachers to individualize their professional development plans and allows schools to use creative ways to improve teaching.

In addition, virtual coaching provides reflective learning opportunities. Through this process teachers engage in systematic reflection, analyzing their instruction and evaluating what can be changed. Teachers reflect in action as coaches provide feedback by improvising and using adaptive strategies to handle unexpected situations. Although there are established learning goals before the observation, real-time feedback requires teachers to engage in inquiry and think spontaneously. These unplanned reflection opportunities prompt critical and flexible thinking in response to classroom situations. This entire process promotes collaboration and in-depth conversation between the virtual coach and teacher.

PRACTICAL IMPLICATIONS

Virtual coaching goes beyond having a peer coach that does not have to be physically present in the classroom. With support from a content expert or teacher peer, teachers can participate in the final step of professional development that is often missed: critical reflection on practice. By focusing on the transfer of training knowledge to the classroom environment, teachers are encouraged to make needed changes in order to enhance classroom instruction. This shared leadership motivates the teacher, is rewarding for the coach, and is beneficial for the school.

Teachers benefit professionally from increased performance based on personalized feedback from the virtual coach. Coaches observe lessons, provide detailed feedback, and offer suggestions in real time. This immediate feedback offers instant interventions as circumstances arise. In addition, teachers have the opportunity to engage in comprehensive discussion with another professional to further understand the feedback provided. This reflective practice allows teachers to identify what went well and areas for improvement. Teachers gain a sense of empowerment through collaboration that is focused on their individualized learning plans.

Teachers also benefit personally, as virtual coaching promotes continuous learning. They are able to reflect and talk about their instruction, which facilitates individual discovery and development. Through this mutual support, both the coach and the teacher experience personal growth from learning new ideas and enhancing their skills.

Although the concept of virtual coaching is easy to implement, it is critical that the coaches themselves possess effective teaching dispositions and strategies to provide guidance and encouragement. Coaches must be competent in best practices and innovative ways to teach content for the age group observed.

The rapport and relationship between the teacher and coach are fundamental for success as feedback must be presented in a positive manner and specialized to address the objectives of the learning agenda. Coaches must be cognizant of the amount of comments and specific directions they communicate with the teacher.

Feedback should be clear and precise to prevent cognitive overload for the teacher. Because they will be responding to classroom encounters live using a Bluetooth device, coaches must have good communication skills and be comfortable with providing immediate corrective feedback. In addition, coaches must also be technology savvy (for example, Skype, Zoom, Google Hangout, Bluetooth devices) and be able to troubleshoot potential connection problems.

Schools gain access to significant resources through virtual coaching. Administrators are able to address specific teacher needs for staff development, and teachers are able to try out new strategies in a nonthreatening environment. Through shared decision making, both the teacher and peer coach profit as they learn from each other. In addition to these benefits, teachers are modeling effective use of technology and communication for students. Because professional development is customized, areas of concern are met, and many people are involved in the improvement of instruction.

SUMMARY

Virtual coaching has many positive aspects. Regardless of time, distance, or money, schools and teachers have access to information, individuals, and resources. Teachers are provided immediate feedback during instruction and are able to analyze teaching with an education colleague after instruction. Teacher competence improves practice, which directly enhances student learning.

Although there are proven benefits, virtual coaching adds additional responsibility to a teacher's role. Due to existing demands (for example, lesson planning, classroom management, documentation, interventions, teaching, grading), teachers are burdened and strained for time. Schools often require teachers to attend professional development based on what administrators deem as important or what is trending in education.

From a teacher's perspective, virtual coaching may be viewed as an administrator's demand rather than as an equal partnership. For this reason, it is crucial that virtual coaching is presented in a manner that solicits teacher buy-in and encourages teacher autonomy. As Thomas et al. (2015) stated, teachers "must feel their opinions and experiences are valued, respected, and used in ways to help them change and grow" (p. 2).

It takes practice to become comfortable with virtual coaching. The ability to process what the coach is recommending while attending to classroom happenings (for example, talking, withitness, content delivery) can be a complicated process. Being able to balance listening to a colleague's suggestions in your ear and implementing those adaptive strategies instantly takes skill and practice.

On the other side, the coach must possess a wealth of instructional strategies and positive dispositions to promote an encouraging and supportive environment. The coach must be confident deciding when to offer feedback and when to allow the teacher to figure things out on his or her own. Also, the nature of the feedback provided (supportive and constructive versus negative and critical) can lead to the success or failure of the relationship.

The success of the virtual coaching experience depends on a teacher's willingness to take initiative in engaging in the process and embracing change. The coach's role is also critical in providing a positive relationship that supports the teacher's needs. Personal and organizational commitment is essential on both sides for this transformational process to work.

QUESTIONS FOR REFLECTION

As schools and educators think about the possibility of utilizing virtual coaching, it may help to reflect on these questions. Reflection on these questions is essential to implement an effective virtual coaching mentorship program that can enhance teacher quality and improve student achievement.

1. How can we develop a collaborative culture that promotes virtual coaching?
2. What type of training (teacher and coach) is required to foster a positive virtual coaching experience?
3. How can teachers be motivated to collaborate with colleagues to support each other in the quest for improvement?
4. What resources (for example, master teachers, equipment, collaborative relationships with other schools) do we currently have to implement virtual coaching? What additional resources do we need?
5. How do we evaluate the effectiveness of the virtual coaching mentorship to assess if it improved classroom instruction and student learning?

Conclusion

Taking Next Steps: A Look to the Future

Patty Kohler-Evans and Debbie Dailey

During the development of this book, as editors, we have sought to closely examine coaching practice through an exploration of myriad coaching applications, for both preservice and in-service educators. While initiated as a simple request for ideas and examples of varied coaching experiences, we received much more than we expected! Our query has resulted in countless creative, multifaceted, boldly applied, and fascinating stories of successful, growth-producing, and results-generating uses of a basic and unwavering set of tried-and-true practices we call coaching.

What we came to realize is that the basic elements of coaching remain intact, while the applications of coaching skills know very few boundaries. Coaching, as we have endeavored to investigate it, is a practice that stays absolutely firm in its definition, its components, and its foundational purpose.

What has changed during the last ten or so years is how coaching takes place, how it is delivered, in what arenas it occurs, and who some of the key coaching players are. We have found that *anyone* can become an effective coach if he or she invests sufficient time and effort to learn, practice, and apply some unique and specific behaviors.

In a traditional sense, the supervisor, superordinate, professor, or school leader has always taken on the role of coach. What we have learned is that the peer, student, candidate, fellow teacher, and colleague can serve just as if not more effectively in the coaching seat.

Technology has no doubt lessened the distance between the coach and the coached, but the basic elemental, powerful, and transformational possibilities for coaching create endless opportunities for educators, whether they are in a one-room schoolhouse or in a contemporary virtual setting. Coaching has tremendous possibilities for teachers, administrators, university instructors, and supervisors. Ultimately, coaching has an amazing potential to transform the lives of the students who are impacted by the instructional decisions that are made each and every day in classrooms across the nation.

In the conclusion to *Coaching Innovations: Providing Instructional Support Anywhere, Anytime*, we revisit essential coaching skills and glance back on some of the potential applications of these critical behaviors. We hope to whet the appetites of our readers by suggesting ways to begin. Finally, as we have in the previous chapters, we will leave by posing some reflective questions for consideration, regardless of the setting, players, or context.

GLANCING BACK

In the introduction, the case for instructional coaching was presented with a reminder that professional development, as it has been practiced for decades, simply does not work! This elemental truth has been reinforced throughout the literature for years. Quite simply, teachers who are asked to make lasting, qualitative, student-impacting change do not do so well without support. One-shot attempts to fill up the time with professional development activities that are not followed up with embedded, ongoing support are ineffective. They waste time, effort, resources, and, most importantly, they yield few if any student results.

Coaching has shown itself to be the missing piece to presentation, theory, demonstration, and practice with feedback (Joyce and Showers, 1995). Coaching emphasizes a collegial relationship based on mutual trust and respect for the purpose of improving instruction.

Coaching is characterized by several key elements; these essentials were examined in chapter 1. The potential impact of a positive, outcome-focused coaching relationship is mind-boggling; however, critical behaviors must be in place. These behaviors include committed listening, paraphrasing, presuming positive intent, and providing reflective feedback. These behaviors take place in a safe, confidential, nonjudgmental, trusting relationship in which both coach and coached are sharing common goals for student achievement. By cradling these skills within a framework of trust, amazing results are possible.

Typically, coaching is regarded as an effective practice that serves to boost student academic performance. In chapter 2, coaching for affective development was introduced as a means to impact and influence classroom culture and climate. The concept of relatedness was discussed, highlighting five key elements: relationship, routines, respect, responsiveness, and rapport. Using these elements as a framework, the coaching relationship is built within a space in which both coach and coached seek to implement best practices within an academically *safe* environment. Embedding the elements of relatedness both in the coaching relationship and the classroom increases the likelihood that this takes place.

In the next two sections of *Coaching Innovations: Providing Instructional Support Anywhere, Anytime*, numerous practices were discussed, and the reader was provided with a host of examples, success stories, ideas for implementation, barriers encountered, and finally questions for reflection. An examination of coaching, both virtually and using face-to-face means, was conducted. In these chapters, innovative ideas were presented and step-by-step experiences were relayed to the reader. Each author reflected on lessons she has learned as she recounts myriad coaching applications. These chapters capture an amazing array of coaching scenarios, each anchored by that which makes coaching powerful: committed, trust-based, nonjudgmental relationships developed for the purpose of helping all students succeed.

LOOKING FORWARD

As we conclude, we would like to challenge our readers to pull from our experiences, learn from our successes and challenges, and take those first (or next) critical steps to implement coaching on some level. Whether it begins with your next conversation, during which you commit to listen intently, or you are exploring the purchase of equipment to facilitate coaching through a virtual setting, we ask that you take that step.

As countless researchers have told us since the beginning of the twenty-first century, coaching, when added to other effective instructional practices, can be a game changer, impacting students' lives in ways previously unimaginable. Here are a few ideas for moving forward.

- Start small, but start. As we know, the longest journey begins with a step. If coaching is a new concept, we suggest you engage in additional development of your own knowledge. There are numerous books on coaching and coaching skills. There are also a host of excellent programs designed to teach the basic coaching skills in a safe, nonthreatening way. Develop a deeper understanding of what coaching is, what it looks like and sounds like, and what it can do for your community.
- Develop a plan of action. As you explore coaching elements and design a clearer definition of what it is and what it isn't, ask yourselves, what do we want to accomplish with our coaching? How do we want to move forward? What key players do we need to involve? Do we want to begin with a grade level? A class? A school? Or within a partnership with our

local teacher training institute? What resources are we aware of? With whom do we need to have the next conversation?
- Remember that technology serves us; we don't serve technology. Much of this book addresses the use of bug in the ear as well as other technology applications. Some schools naturally gravitate to technology because of proximity and other issues. Others have different areas of focus. Technology is amazing, time saving, and limitless in its potential uses; however, your team may not be ready to buy new equipment so that you can try out virtual coaching. Remember that technology is a tool to enhance coaching but it is not a necessity to *coach*.
- Finally, enjoy yourself and be as creative as you wish to be. Above all else, we encourage our readers to have fun along the journey. Coaching can lead to tremendous insights and revelations about ourselves, our beliefs, our hopes, and our apprehensions. When we enter into trusting relationships as we seek to serve our students in better ways, the journey itself can be exhilarating. Layering our current collegial collaborations with new conversations enhances the lives of all of us, especially our students.

As we conclude, we wish to leave our readers with a few final questions.

QUESTIONS FOR REFLECTION

1. What current coaching practices are used in your school community?
2. What words would you use to describe your current coaching reality?
3. What words would you like to use to describe your coaching reality?
4. One year from now, how would you like to describe coaching in your school community?
5. How would you characterize yourself as a coach?
6. How might coaching better serve your students?
7. How might virtual coaching positively impact your students?
8. Which of the practices, stories, and scenarios shared in this book resonate with you?
9. If you were to take one step toward improving your coaching practice, what would that step be?

Now take that critical step.

References

Ackland, R. (1991). A review of the peer coaching literature. *Journal of Staff Development, 12*, 22–26.
Allen, M. (2014). Catching the bug: How virtual coaching improves teaching. *Educational Horizons, 92*(4), 25–27.
Aguilar, E. (2013). *The art of coaching: Effective strategies for school transformation*. San Francisco, CA: Jossey-Bass.
Appleton, K. (2008). Developing science pedagogical content knowledge through mentoring elementary teachers. *Journal of Science Teacher Education, 19*, 523–45. doi:10.1007/s10972-008-9109-4
Arya, P., Christ, T., and Chiu, M. (2013). Facilitation of teacher behaviors: An analysis of literacy teachers' video-case discussions. *Journal of Teacher Education, 65*(2), 111–27.
Association for Talent Development (ATD). (n.d.). *Essentials of developing a mentoring program*. Retrieved from https://www.td.org/Education/Programs/Developing-a-Mentoring-Program
Bandura, A. (1977). Self-efficacy: Toward a unifying theory of behavior change. *Psychological Review, 84*(2), 191–215.
Bandura, A. (1989). Regulation of cognitive processes through perceived self-efficacy. *Developmental Psychology, 25*, 725–39.
Barkley, S. G. (2005). *Quality teaching in a culture of coaching*. Lanham, MD: Rowman & Littlefield.
Bearwald, R. R. (2011). It's about the questions. *Educational Leadership, 69*(2), 74–77.
Benson, T. R., and Cotabish, A. A. (2014). Virtual bugs: An innovative peer coaching intervention to improve the instructional behaviors of teacher candidates. *Southeastern Regional Association of Teacher Educators Journal, Fall/Winter, 24*(1), 1–9.
Betz, A. (2015). It's not (just) about the "aha!" moment. *Coaching World, 2015*(16), 22–23. Retrieved from https://www.joomag.com/magazine/coaching-world-issue-16-november-2015/0974226001448373239?page=11
Blackman, A. (2010). Coaching as a leadership development tool for teachers. *Professional Development in Education, 36*(3), 421–41.
Bowman, C., and McCormick, S. (2000). Comparison of peer coaching versus traditional supervision effects. *Journal of Educational Research, 93*(4), 256–62.
Burley-Allen, M. (1995). *Listening: The forgotten skill*. Second edition. New York: John Wiley & Sons, Inc.
Butler, D. L., Lauscher, H. N., Jarvis-Selinger, S., and Bekingham, B. (2004). Collaboration and self-regulation in teachers' professional development. *Teaching and Teacher Education, 20*(50), 435–55.

Coaching for Results Global. (2013). *Powerful coaching: Level II.*
Comer, J. (2004). *Leave no child behind: Preparing today's youth for tomorrow's world.* New Haven, CT: Yale University Press.
Conway, P. F., and Clark, C. M. (2003). The journey inward and outward: A re-examination of Fuller's concerns-based model of teacher development. *Teaching and Teacher Education, 19*(5), 465–82.
Cotabish, A., Dailey, D., Robinson, A., and Hughes, A. (2013). The effects of a STEM intervention on elementary students' science knowledge and skills. *School Science and Mathematics, 113*(5), 215–26.
Council for the Accreditation of Educator Preparation (CAEP). (2015). *Standards.* Retrieved from http://www.caepnet.org/
Covey, S. R. (1989). *The seven habits of highly effective people: Powerful lessons in personal change.* New York: Simon & Schuster.
Dailey, D., and Robinson, A. (2016). Elementary teachers: Concerns about implementing a science program. *School Science and Mathematics, 116*(3), 139–47.
Dailey, D., and Robinson, A. (2017). Improving and sustaining elementary teachers science teaching perceptions and process skills: A post intervention study. *Journal of Science Teacher Education, 28*(2), 169–85.
Danielson, C. (2007). *Enhancing professional practice: A framework for teaching.* Alexandria, VA: Association for Supervision and Curriculum Development.
Danielson, C., Axtell, D., Bevan. P., Cleland, B., McKay, C., Phillips, E., and Wright, K. (2009). *Implementing the framework for teaching in enhancing professional practice: ASCD action tool.* Alexandria, VA: Association for Supervision and Curriculum Development.
Darling-Hammond, L. (2010). Teacher education and the American future. *Journal of Teacher Education, 61*(1–2), 35–47.
Davis, B., and Waite, S. (2006). The longer term effects of a public school/state university induction program. *The Professional Educator, 29*(2). Retrieved from www.theprofessionaleducator.org
Dweck, C. S. (2014). *Mindset: The new psychology of success.* New York: Ballantine Books.
Emory University (n.d.). The story of "Mentor." Learning and Organizational Development Human Resources. Retrieved from http://www.learningservices.emory.edu/mentor_emory/mentorstory.html
Gallavan, N. P. (2007). Seven perceptions influencing novice teachers' efficacy and cultural competence. *Journal of Praxis in Multicultural Education, 2*(1), 6–22.
Gallavan, N. P. (2016). If you want your students to change, then you need to change: Mediating the sources and benefits of teacher self-efficacy with teacher candidates. In T. Petty, A. Good, and M. Putman (Eds.), *Handbook of research on professional development for quality teaching and learning* (pp. 324–45). Hersey, PA: IGI Global.
Gilles, C., Wilson, J., and Eaton, M. (2009). Sustaining teachers' growth and renewal through action research, induction programs and collaboration. *Teacher Education Quarterly, 37*(1), 91–108.
Goldrick, L., Osta, D., Barlin, D., and Burn, J. (2012). *Review of state policies on teacher induction.* Santa Cruz, CA: New Teacher Center. Retrieved from www.newteachercenter.org
Gottman, J. M. (2001). *The relationship cure: A five-step guide for building better connections with family, friends, and lovers.* New York: Crown.
Guskey, T. R. (1986). Staff development and the process of teacher change. *Educational Researcher, 15*(5), 5–12.
Gustafson, B., Guilbert, S., and MacDonald, D. (2002). Beginning elementary science teachers: Developing professional knowledge during a limited mentoring experience. *Research in Science Education, 32*(3), 281–302.
Hill, E. (2017). *Culminating project 1: Stop-animation video.* Retrieved from http://betterlesson.com/lesson/633451/intro-for-culminating-project-1-stop-animation-video-day-1-of-project
International Coach Federation. (n.d.). *Core competencies.* Retrieved January 25, 2017, from http://www.coachfederation.org/credential/landing.cfm?ItemNumber=2206

Isenberg, J., McCreadie, J., Durham, J., and Pearson, B. (2009). *Changing education through the arts: Final evaluation report, 2005–2008.* Fairfax, VA: George Mason University, College of Education and Human Development.
John F. Kennedy Center for Performing Arts. (2008). *Key features of the Kennedy Center's changing education through the arts (CETA) model school program.* Retrieved from https://www.kennedy-center.org/education/ceta/Key_Features_of_indiv_Teachers.pdf
Jones, A. (n.d.). *Coaching vs. mentoring: What works best for teachers.* Retrieved from https://www.theguardian.com/teacher-network/teacher-blog/2014/aug/05/coaching-mentoring-teachers-professional-development
Joyce, B., and B. Showers. (1981). Transfer of training: The contribution of coaching. *Journal of Education, 163,* 163–72.
Joyce, B., and B. Showers. (1995). *Student achievement through staff development: Fundamentals of school renewal.* Second edition. White Plains, NY: Longman.
Joyce, B., and Showers, B. (1996). The evolution of peer coaching. *Educational Leadership, 53*(6), 12–16.
Kain, E. (2011). President Obama says standardized tests make education boring, don't adequately measure performance. *Forbes.* Retrieved from http://tinyurl.com/jer42gb
Kee, K., Anderson, K., Dearing, V., Harris, E., and Shuster, F. (2010). *Results coaching: The new essential for school leaders.* Thousand Oaks, CA: Corwin Press.
Killion, J., and Harrison, C. (2006). *Taking the lead: New roles for teachers and school-based coaches.* Oxford, OH: National Staff Development Council.
Knight, J. (2007). *Instructional coaching: A partnership approach to improving instruction.* Thousand Oaks, CA: Corwin Press.
Knight, J. (2011). What good coaches do. *Educational Leadership, 69*(2), 18–22.
Kretlow, A. G., Cooke, N. L., and Wood, C. L. (2012). Using in-service and coaching to increase teachers' accurate use of research-based strategies. *Remedial and Special Education, 33*(6), 348–61.
Kurtts, S. A., and Levin, B. B. (2000). Using peer-coaching with preservice teachers to develop reflective practice and collegial support. *Teaching Education, 11*(3), 297–310. DOI: 10.1080/713698980
Lutrick, E., and Szabo, S. (2012). Instructional leaders' beliefs about effective professional development. *The Delta Kappa Gamma Bulletin, 78*(3), 6–12.
Lynch, P. (2007). Making meaning many ways: An exploratory look at integrating the arts with classroom curriculum. *Art Education, 60*(4), 33–38.
Maxwell, J. C. (2008). *Leadership gold: Lessons I've learned from a lifetime of leading.* Nashville, TN: Thomas Nelson.
McAllister, E. A., and Neubert, G. A. (1995). *New teacher helping new teachers: Preservice peer-coaching.* Bloomington, IN: Edinfo Press.
McTighe, J., and Wiggins, G. (2013). *Essential questions: Opening doors to student understanding.* Alexandria, VA: Association for Supervision and Curriculum Development.
Miller, R., Wake, D., and Whittingham, J. (2015). Integrating the arts with the Arkansas A+ model. *Arkansas Association of Instructional Media Journal, 48*(1), 14–17.
Miller, R., Wake, D., and Whittingham, J. (2016). *The content and construct development of the PACT Survey.* Paper presented at the Annual Meeting of the American Educational Research Association, Washington, DC.
National Board of Professional Teaching Standards (2016). *Five core propositions.* Retrieved from http://www.nbpts.org/five-core-propositions
National Center for Education Statistics. (2008). *Schools and staffing survey.* Retrieved from http://nces.ed.gov/surveys/sass/index.asp
National Governors Association Center for Best Practices. (2010). *Common core state standards, mathematics.* National Governors Association Center for Best Practices, Council of Chief State School Officers, Washington, DC. Retrieved from http://www.corestandards.org/Math/Content/HSG/SRT/
NGSS Lead States. (2013). *Next generation science standards: For states, by states.* Washington, DC: The National Academies Press. Retrieved from https://www.nextgenscience.org/dci-arrangement/hs-ps1-matter-and-its-interactions

Parker, T. S., Barnes, C. D., and Kohler-Evans, P. (2016). *Success favors well-prepared teachers: Developing routines and relationships to improve school culture.* Lanham, MD: Rowman & Littlefield Publishing.

Ponte, J. P., and Chapman, O. (2008). Preservice mathematics teachers' knowledge and development. In L. English (Ed.), *Handbook of international research in mathematics education* (pp. 225–36). New York: Routledge.

Owen, H. D. (2015). Making the most of mobility: Virtual mentoring and education practitioner professional development. *Research in Learning Technology, 23,* 255–66. http://dx.doi.org/10.3402/rlt.v23.25566

Robbins, P. (1991). *How to plan and implement a peer coaching program.* Alexandria, VA: Association for Supervision and Curriculum Development.

Rock, D. (2006). *Quiet leadership.* New York: HarperCollins.

Rock, M. L., Gregg, M., Howard, P. W., Ploessl, D. M., Maughn, S., Gable, R. A., and Zigmond, N. P. (2009). See me, hear me, coach me virtual bug-in-ear technology brings immediacy to professional development. *National Staff Development Council, 30*(3), 24–32.

Rogers, S., and Renard, L. (1999). Relationship-driven teaching. *Educational Leadership, 57*(1), 34–37.

Scheeler, M. C., Congdon, M., and Stansbery, S. (2010). Providing immediate feedback to co-teachers through bug-in-ear technology: An effective method of peer coaching in inclusion classrooms. *Teacher Education and Special Education: The Journal of the Teacher Education Division of the Council for Exceptional Children, 33*(1), 83–96.

Scott, S. (2002). *Fierce conversations: Achieving success at work & in life, one conversation at a time.* New York: Berkley Books.

Sharplin, E. J., Stahl, G., and Kerhwald, B. (2016). It's about improving my practice: The learner experience of real-time coaching. *Australian Journal of Teacher Education, 41*(5), 118–35. Retrieved from http://ro.ecu.edu.au/ajte/vol41/iss5/8

Showers, B. (1982). *Transfer of training: The contribution of coaching* (Report No. ED 231 035). Eugene, OR: Center for Educational Policy and Management, College of Education, University of Oregon.

Showers, B. (1984). *Peer coaching: A strategy for facilitating transfer of training* (Report No. ED 271 849). Eugene, OR: Center for Educational Policy and Management, College of Education, University of Oregon.

Showers, B., and Joyce, B. (1996). The evolution of peer coaching. *Educational Leadership, 53*(6), 12–16.

Silverstein, L. B. & Layne, S.(2014). What is arts integration? Explore the Kennedy Center's comprehensive definition. *The Kennedy Center: ARTSEDGE-the National Arts and Education Network.*

Sousa, D. A., and Pilecki, T. (2013). *From STEM to STEAM: Using brain-compatible strategies to integrate the arts.* Thousand Oaks, CA: Sage Publications.

Sparks, D. (2006). *Leading for results: Transforming teaching, learning, and relationships in schools.* Thousand Oaks, CA: Corwin Press.

Swafford, J., Maltsberger, A., Button, K., and Furgerson, P. (1997). Peer coaching for facilitating effective literacy instruction. In C. K. Kinzer, K. A. Hinchman, and D. J. Leu (Eds.), *Inquiries in literacy theory and practice: Forty-sixth yearbook of the National Reading Conference* (pp. 416–26). Chicago: National Reading Conference.

Sweeney, D. (2011). *Student-centered coaching: A guide for K–8 coaches and principals.* Thousand Oaks, CA: Corwin Press.

Tavanyar, J. (2014). Lost in cyberspace? *Coaching World,* 8–9. Retrieved from https://www.joomag.com/en/newsstand/coaching-world-issue-12-november-2014/0547505001416845717

Thomas, E. E., Bell, D. L., Spelman, M., and Briody, J. (2015). The growth of instructional coaching partner conversations in a preK–3rd grade teacher professional development experience. *Journal of Adult Education, 44*(2), 1–6.

UCA College of Education. (2015). *COE Conceptual framework.* University of Central Arkansas. Retrieved from https://uca.edu/education/conceptualframework/

Wake, D., Dailey, D., Cotabish, A., and Benson, T. (in press). Virtual bugs and coaching: Teacher candidate's perceptions and concerns regarding on-demand corrective feedback. *Journal of Technology and Teacher Education.*

Wiggins, G., and McTighe, J. (2005). *Understanding by design.* Second edition. Alexandria, VA: Association for Supervision and Curriculum Development.

Zeichner, K. (2010). Rethinking the connections between campus courses and field experiences in college- and university-based teacher education. *Journal of Teacher Education, 61*(1–2), 89–99.

Zordak, S. E. (2016). *Triangle classification.* National Council of Teachers of Mathematics. Retrieved from https://illuminations.nctm.org/Lesson.aspx?id=2195

About the Editors

Debbie Dailey, EdD, is an assistant professor of teaching and learning at the University of Central Arkansas, where she is the coordinator for the Gifted and Talented Program. Formerly, Debbie served as the curriculum coordinator and peer coach of a Javits-funded program, STEM Starters, which focused on improving science instruction in the elementary grades. Through this program, Debbie coached elementary teachers implementing problem-based learning science units in their classroom.

Prior to moving to higher education, Debbie was a high school science teacher and gifted education teacher for twenty years. Debbie has authored and co-authored multiple publications including journal articles, books, book chapters, and products focused on K–12 STEM and gifted education. She has delivered numerous professional development workshops and presentations at local, state, national, and international venues. Debbie currently serves as the secretary for the Council for Exceptional Children—The Association for the Gifted (CEC-TAG) and is a selected member of the Professional Standards Committee for the National Association for Gifted Children.

Patty Kohler-Evans, EdD, is a professor in the Elementary, Literacy, and Special Education Department at the University of Central Arkansas. She has nineteen years of experience as a special education administrator in the largest district in Arkansas, serving urban students with numerous needs stemming from poverty, disability, and race. She is a member of the International Coaching Federation and has served as an executive coach for numerous school principals in the Little Rock School District during the past eight years. She provides professional development to educators through virtual as well as face-to-face settings.

This is Patty's fourth book, and she has written extensively on inclusive practice in schools. Patty currently serves as director of the UCA Mashburn Center for Learning, which seeks to ensure that all teachers in Arkansas have access to methodologies that meet the needs of struggling learners in K–12 schools.

About the Contributors

Candice Dowd Barnes, EdD, is an associate professor and the interim chair at the University of Central Arkansas for the Department of Elementary, Literacy, and Special Education. She is also the chief operations officer for Parker Education and Development, LLC. She strongly believes in the power of authentic learning experiences to teach beyond the walls of the classroom into all aspects of life. Dr. Barnes has an extensive background in early childhood education, curriculum and assessment planning, and educational leadership. She is a dynamic speaker and accomplished author of multiple articles on developing authentic relationships and interactions with individuals of diverse and unique backgrounds and histories, service learning, and social and emotional development. Dr. Barnes has also presented across the country on various topics related to the concept of coaching for change, change enterprise, relatedness skill development, and social and cultural capital.

Tammy R. Benson, EdD, is currently a professor and department chairperson of the Department of Teaching and Learning in the College of Education at the University of Central Arkansas, where she has led a dynamic faculty for six years. Before that, she served as director of an award-winning graduate program, the Master of Arts in Teaching licensure program. Dr. Benson received a doctoral degree from the University of Memphis in curriculum and instruction with an emphasis in early childhood education. She has two degrees from the University of Central Arkansas including a master's degree in reading with a reading specialist endorsement and a bachelor's degree in elementary education. Dr. Benson maintains a strong research agenda that includes mentoring, reading intervention strategies (specifically dyslexia training), leadership and its impact on quality teacher education programs and K–12 schools, instructional technology (specifically the bug in ear approach to coaching and internship supervision), outreach programs that connect UCA teacher education students and positively benefit K–12 at-risk learners, and excellence in teaching, including service learning. Her total years of teaching, research, and service to the University of Central Arkansas total twenty-six. Before that she was a classroom teacher for five years, where she implemented best practices in early childhood education.

Michelle Buchanan, MAT, NBCT, has been teaching for eighteen years. She taught fourteen years of junior high science and engineering, and she received many national awards for her teaching, curriculum, and lessons in science and gifted instruction—TED-Ed Distinguished Educator, PBS Innovative Teacher Award, Edward C. Roy National Teacher of the Year, and U.S. Department of Education's Star Teaching Award, to name a few. Buchanan is currently working on her PhD in leadership studies at the University of Central Arkansas. She received her master's degree from Louisiana College in Pineville and her bachelor of science degree from the University of North Texas in Denton. She teaches courses on project-based instruction that incorporates edtech, classroom diversity and differentiation, and educational psychology and pedagogy for STEMTeach. Her research interests include STEM education with teacher education, education technology, and differentiated instruction.

Nancy P. Gallavan, PhD, is a professor of teacher education at the University of Central Arkansas. She earned her PhD at the University of Denver, her master's at the University of Colorado, and her bachelor of science at Southwest Missouri State University. As part of the Master of Arts in Teaching (MAT) program, Nancy specializes in classroom assessment, cultural competence, and social studies education. Additionally, she supervises interns, chairs multiple dissertation committees, and serves as the UCA academic liaison to institutional diversity and co-counselor of the UCA CoE chapter of Kappa Delta Pi. With 160+ publications in peer-reviewed books and journals, Nancy is also active in the American Educational Research Association, the Association of Teacher Education, Kappa Delta Pi, the National Association for Multicultural Education, and the National Council for the Social Studies. She has received awards for her teaching, scholarship, and service in her college, at her university, and with national associations. She is a past president and distinguished member of the Association of Teacher Educators and an inaugural member of the Eleanor Roosevelt Legacy Chapter of Kappa Delta Pi.

Dr. Victoria Groves-Scott, EdD, is the dean for the College of Education and professor of special education at the University of Central Arkansas

(UCA). She received her doctorate in special education from the University of Kansas in 1995. Dr. Groves-Scott received the Teaching Excellence Award from Southern Illinois University Edwardsville in 2006 and the 2006 Emerson Excellence in Teaching Award. She was chosen by her peers as the Kansas Council for Exceptional Children Outstanding Special Education Teacher of the Year for 1998 and was also awarded the Council for Exceptional Children Federation Award in 1999. She has conducted research in the areas of assessment, phonemic awareness, reading instruction, instructional technology, diversity, and assistive technology.

Nykela Jackson, PhD, is an assistant professor of teaching and learning at the University of Central Arkansas. She earned a PhD in higher education administration and an MEd in gifted education from the University of Southern Mississippi. Dr. Jackson has worked in public schools (elementary/middle levels, gifted education, and instructional technology) and education administration (curriculum and assessment). Her research interests include culturally responsive teaching, differentiated instruction, and STEM education.

Rachelle Miller, PhD, is currently an assistant professor in the Department of Teaching and Learning at the University of Central Arkansas. She received her PhD from Purdue University in educational psychology with an emphasis in gifted education. She currently collaborates with Arkansas A+ Schools by completing program evaluation and assisting in the development of arts-integrated curriculum in their participating schools. Her research interests include supporting the academic needs of low-income gifted students, integrating the arts into the general and gifted curriculum, and examining teacher perceptions of arts integration.

Donna Wake, EdD, is the associate dean in the University of Central Arkansas College of Education and an associate professor in the Department of Teaching and Learning. Her doctorate is from Temple University in curriculum, instruction, and technology with an emphasis on K–12 literacy. She has earned master's in education from La Salle University in Philadelphia, a master's in art history from the University of Arkansas Little Rock, and a bachelor's in English from Hendrix College in Conway, Arkansas. Her research interests include teacher education, teacher education reform, multiliteracies, and education technology.

www.ingramcontent.com/pod-product-compliance
Lightning Source LLC
Chambersburg PA
CBHW021847220426
43663CB00005B/431